Often the sweeping tides of grief send torrential tears and crashing waves of regret and sadness. Bishop Andrew Turner's thoughtful book *After* is a guiding light for those who have walked through or become lodged in the valley of the shadow of death! Give it as a guide to the grief stricken.

Bishop T. D. Jakes
CEO, TDJ Enterprises
New York Times best-selling author

"We loved them but God loved them best" is a statement many of us have heard after the loss of a loved one. This statement, while at the core, means well, I was always confused by it. The statement "We loved them but God loved them best" seems to suggest that God loves the ones who get to heaven before the rest of us so much that he would take them away from us. Losing a loved one is painful and confusing and a host of emotions no one has been able to fully describe ... until now! Bishop Andrew Turner gives the clearest and most personal insight in *After* many of us will ever read. One of my favorite lines in this incredibly consoling book sums it up well: "*After* is not just a word; no, it's your road map ..."

Bishop Lester Love

It was the great championship boxer Joe Louis who said, "Everybody wants to go to heaven, but nobody wants to die." When grief shatters our world and the pain of death consumes us, we not only want comfort, but we want answers. Where do we find the strength to face the complex reality that the presence of pain is not always a sign of trouble, but a corridor to a transformational beginning?

How do you respond to the question "What makes you so strong?" when you should be in the fetal position from the overwhelming weight of your circumstances? These questions are answered in the book *After*. Andrew Turner helps us to see that death, pain, and loss at their core are more than a debilitating phenomenon; they are conduits used to reignite our hope in a God who is greater than our circumstances!

I promise you that if you can find your way through the commonplaces of your life, this book will help you to reach an unconventional place of power that will push you to a new beginning.

Reverend Jamal Harrison Bryant
Pastor, Empowerment Temple

After offers not just a glimmer but the bright illumination of hope. So whether you are crawling, limping, or barely moving, you will find that this book will help you make it through the darkest parts of the journey. *After* is your place of triumph, and I look forward to seeing you there!

Reverend Dr. Marilyn Monroe Harris
Pastor, First Baptist Church of Teaneck

After defines where Andrew Turner used to be. But more than anything, it reveals where he has chosen to be today. If you've experienced the pangs of grief because of death, then you're a prime candidate for what you're about to read.

Bishop Henry Fernandez
Faith Center Ministries

Navigating the course of grief is an inevitable eventuality that each of us will experience. How we traverse the terrain of sorrowful transitions is predicated upon the strategic utilization of life skills aimed toward the holistic well-being of spirit, body, and mind. *After* is not only a requisite tool for the journey, but a vital resource for growth and preparation for those experiencing the challenges associated with grief and transition. Andrew Turner masterfully guides us through his process from tragedy to triumph with biblical truth and transparency.

Dr. Craig L. Oliver, Sr.
Pastor, Elizabeth Baptist Church

After

Finding Your Passion & Purpose for What's Next

ANDREW C. TURNER II

Foreword by Joseph W. Walker III

Dedication

To those unknown broken men and women who are willing to
give life another shot, knowing they are not alone

After: Finding Your Passion & Purpose for What's Next

Copyright 2019 Andrew C. Turner II

Print ISBN 9781683593171
Digital ISBN 9781683593140

Contents

Foreword

—

T here are moments in all our lives when we are blindsided by the unexpected. Life is filled with challenges, and often our resilience is put to the test. So many people are unable to bounce back from setbacks because they don't know where to begin. This book is an incredible and insightful guide that charts a course for recovery. It is rare to read a book so transparent yet filled with practical application.

I know personally what it's like to experience trauma in life. The question that was raised in my spirit was, *What next?* It is a universal question that seeks to discover what will become of us "after" the events have shaken our foundation and threatened the normalcy of our lives. Like Jeremiah I've felt consumed in the moment of my pain and wanted to walk away. Like Job, I've questioned God. Like David I've been in dark places wondering where God was. All of us have been there. What provides hope for us all is that God has plans for our lives *after*. Like Job we are poised for double for our trouble. Bishop Turner has masterfully crafted a book that gives step-by-step principles to help you recover from life's misfortunes and realize the awesome potential that exists in your future. This book is about working through painful seasons and embracing new ones. There are some great books out, and this is one; however, I also feel this is a necessary book for anyone serious about moving forward into greater things. No matter what has been, the rest of you will be the best of you. You've survived the worst; now the best is yet to come. I'm excited about what happens *After*. If you are too, this is your kind of book. Read it and your life will never be the same.

Bishop Joseph W. Walker III
Senior Pastor, Mt. Zion Baptist Church

INTRODUCTION

—— *After* Is Not Just a Word ——

By itself, the word *after* doesn't seem to mean much. In the Bible we don't learn a great deal from its Greek or Hebrew translations. In writing, its use doesn't signal any particular literary excellence. But in your life, the word *after* could be the difference between the old life and the new.

After is not just a two-syllable word; it is a tool to manage your future. Perhaps the course of your life has been altered with one unforeseen event or mishap. That event might have brought you to your knees, causing unbearable pressure and creating physiological, social, spiritual, and emotional trauma. Perhaps the pressures of life have led to stagnation and left you believing that restoration and victory is impossible. You've gone into survival mode. How do you carry on?

You, my friend, are about to discover the moment in time I call *after*, the critical point that determines how your life is rebuilt. Even as you survey the wreckage, you face an all-important choice: give up, or determine what is required to survive. If you embrace your *after*, using everything it has to offer, you will not only survive but thrive in the next chapter of your life.

I

In the many *afters* I've personally experienced—after deaths, failures, and disasters of all kinds—I've discovered a simple formula for moving ahead when you feel you have no choices:

Purpose + Patience = *After*

In this book, I will show you that moving through your *after* doesn't have to be frightening or uncertain; in fact, you can rely on a systematic process and guide to finding value in every experience. How? By redirecting pain into passion. You *can* build and maintain a new desire for life. The following pages will guide you one small, manageable step at a time, until you gather the courage to refuse defeat. With direction and patience, soon you will find yourself walking forward with determination into life *after*.

Outlasting the Storm

Even the best-laid plans and soundest structures have fallen victim to unforeseen events. One such event—a hurricane Katrina, Harvey, or Maria, for example—can cripple a nation, leaving debris and utter darkness. Storms are not biased toward one group of people, bypassing another. These hurricanes were destructive to entire communities with no regard to status or quality of life. The poor and wealthy alike faced turbulent times, with or without insurance. In the same way, life produces disasters for everyone, no matter who you are. And when a disaster hits, it gives us a common platform of pain, sorrow, and suffering.

That is why finding an *after* is equally valuable to all, regardless of ethnic, social, or religious persuasion. We all must walk through similar stages before recovering.

When we observe the path and the aftermath of a natural disaster like a hurricane, we can learn much about survival after life's storms. From a change in pressure, to the storm itself, to recovery, cleanup, and rebuilding, we can respond to our personal disasters just as deliberately as we would a natural disaster. It all starts with a shift in the weather.

The Clouds Roll In

Just days before Katrina hit in 2015, New Orleans residents were enjoying hot, sunny weather with barely a breeze. Weather forecasts on August 25 predicted a 20 percent chance of rain with balmy weekend temperatures. But winds shifted, and so did their future. Just days later, the storm would sweep destruction over the city, and residents would flee for their lives. The difference between their "before" and "after" was almost inconceivable. Everything can change in a shockingly short amount of time.

Life before your personal storm might have been ideal, marked by peace, tranquility, health, and prosperity. Like a family planning a backyard barbecue that August weekend, perhaps your circumstances gave you a sense of safety or accomplishment. But then the winds turned, and everything seemed to change in an instant. A "shift" in life is capable of rendering great leaders, communities, families, entrepreneurs, and, yes, a ministry paralyzed. *After* is your exit plan—your motivation to preserve your life in the face of a storm.

On the other side of the country, someone watching a hurricane report through CNN lenses is in a completely different situation than someone facing the flood. Observers can leave the flood simply by changing channels, but that option isn't available to those facing ground-level devastation. *After* is not a concept for channel surfers; it is for those on the ground. If you are knee-deep in your floodwaters, this book is here to impart life-bringing information and alternatives to surrendering to the storm and being taken by the flood.

Why do you need to find your *after*? *After* redirects your life. *After* weighs hope against hopelessness, knowing death is no longer an option where life is available. Hope will grow from strategic decisiveness, dedicated prayer, and personal commitment. *After* chooses to rebuild on that hope while others offer excuses, becoming victims to storms.

Floods Rise

If your life looks as if it's been hit with a hurricane of trouble or flooded with a swamp of stagnation, this book is your strategic recovery plan before FEMA support and following a few nights in a shelter. You will come to a transitional moment when you must learn how to react to the floodwaters. This will require a shift in your thinking.

Recovering from a flood is even more difficult when resources are scarce. In the same way, our minds often flood with thoughts of our disaster, seeking to find hope in the face of catastrophic domestic challenges, ministry failures, financial peril, or even cancer that takes the life of a loved one. We need tools—resources—to regain focus. Without these tools, we struggle to do the practical things we need to do to carry on, whether it's reaching sales quotas or obtaining a home loan, taking care of a home or supporting children, or seeking to shift a mind or guide a ministry. As you face floods in your mind, use the tools of identifying and unmasking enemy thoughts and making decisive change. These tools are essential to identifying and neutralizing defeated dark thoughts, and finding guidance to make decisive changes. In the coming pages, we will discuss these tools for renewing your mind in depth. They will equip you to begin building again, draining away unhealthy waters, and preparing the ground for new construction.

Help and Rebuilding

At the time of this writing, humanitarian aid for recent hurricane or earthquake victims in Mexico, Florida, Puerto Rico, and Houston, Texas, remains in effect, and residents will need it for an unpredictable period of time. These perils have dampened communities. How will they rebuild their economies? Of course, help and handouts are welcomed, but finding a divine hand-up is necessary for those in search of *after*. We need help in times of decimation, and seeking out the right kind of help and investment makes it possible not only to build, but to build better than before.

Your hand-up comes not only in prayer and support from others, but in valuable practical advice. Your "humanitarian aid" can come in the form of wisdom in the area of wealth, prosperity, and even personal rebranding—specifically tailored to work during the earthquakes or floods of life. While there are plenty of books about these subjects on shelves across our nation, few of them specifically address how to rebrand yourself in the face of life's disasters. But in your *after*, you can choose to initiate recovery on this and every level. From the business world, you can learn to implement simple recovery processes. Yes, even after shattering moments, even after years of stagnation, you can prepare to grow. Each reader must continue to pursue *after*, because life is much greater than a flood.

Life does offer alternatives and aid to flood victims, but intimate aid is required to assist wounded leaders or those suffering from divorce, sickness, ministry challenges, or past mistakes. Rebuilding requires removing wreckage and waste, and that takes courage and commitment. As Nehemiah removed the rubbish prior to rebuilding Jerusalem, in our minds and in our lives, debris must be moved to rebuild to be better and stronger. This labor-intensive task is unavoidable, but it creates hope, and before long a new, stable life will replace shattered memories. So it shall be in your *after*.

Your *After* Is About to Begin

After is not just a word; no, it's your road map, regardless of your religious persuasion, race, creed, or gender. At some point, because of life's systematic structure, both leaders and followers will need to engage an *after*; so will dreamers and business owners, lay members, husbands, wives, family members, and everyone who faces life's inequities and tragedies. Each reader of this work must not cease in pursuing *after*, because life shall become greater than our flood. How am I so sure of this process? My many adversities—along with purpose—have created this work. It is a global tool to restore your hope, your desire for love, and your passion for life and family.

Recently I requested a time-out from life to evaluate what appeared to be an unjust flood; I had faced an extraordinary number of near-crushing challenges. After experiencing the death of loved ones, dreams, finances, and future plans, I needed to find a way to stop giving way to death, become inspired, and regain purpose. Though at times, I'll admit, I wished to peacefully transition from life to death, given all the blows I had sustained, instead I found a path to my own *after*. I rejected death's invitation, and I found that the floods produced character and strength. Just ask Noah. Better yet, ask yourself. Are you better or bitter after your flood? Better is for your *after*; bitterness will cause death. How often do we live with unforgiveness without knowing it breeds bitterness or toxicity? Kirk Franklin, a renowned gospel artist, was given up for adoption as an infant. He recently traveled to visit his biological father, who was dying. Franklin admitted he needed to forgive his father before he left this earth because he could not afford to minister while he was bitter.

Your situation may not be fair, but *fair* is relative when seeking strength or direction for recovery. Our heavenly Father does not operate in human terms of fairness. He develops us through storms. While others see failure, He sees a future. There is a greater plan for your life, beginning with the steps outlined in this book.

In God's Word, the apostle Paul encouraged the Philippians to press on, using a three-part approach that is perfectly suited to life *after*. He wrote:

> Forgetting what is behind and straining toward what is ahead,
> I press on toward the goal to win the prize for which God has
> called me heavenward in Christ Jesus. (Philippians 3:13–14 NIV)

That three-part approach inspired the three parts of this book. First, we *forget what is behind*. In part one of this book you'll discover what to do in the immediate aftermath of a disaster, how to regroup, and how to leave the past in the past. Next, we *strain toward what is ahead.* Part two explores how to come to terms with who we are now and what to do to build hope for the future. This establishes individualized purpose. Our inspirational purpose often achieves its full potential following these dark moments in life. Finally, in part three we *press on toward the goal* with endurance. King David asked God if he should pursue his enemies while his family and loved ones were held captive. His flood was personal; your flood is too. The Lord directed David; pursue while facing opposition, including severe adversity. Indecision, procrastination, and fear will impact movement. Your decision to move is powerful; it overtakes intimidations. Press forward—it will bring enormous value and victory.

While we never lose hope of heaven, let's reach purpose and achieve victories upon this earth until then. As long as you draw breath, you can walk into a victorious *after* in the days ahead.

Let's take this journey together and build better than before. Now is your time to reach up and become one who has weathered devastation, become confident in your present, and enjoy life with a rich *after.*

PART 1

Forgetting What Is Behind

—— ✸ ——

*Brothers and sisters, I do not consider myself yet to have taken hold of it. But one thing I do: **Forgetting what is behind** and straining toward what is ahead, I press on toward the goal to win the prize for which God has called me heavenward in Christ Jesus.*

Philippians 3:13–14 NIV

CHAPTER 1

——————— Sorrow to Joy ———————

We celebrate life with milestones. From conception through our final breath, significant events give way to celebrations. We celebrate at will without limitation. It starts early, even before birth, when an unborn child is celebrated by its parents and well-wishers. You may have attended what's known as a "gender reveal party," where an expecting mother reveals whether she's having a boy or a girl, often with elaborate refreshments, balloons, cakes, and music. She is surrounded by eager friends and family, all waiting with bated breath for the announcement. This new tradition is yet another celebration of the beginning of life.

The new life of an infant brings tears of joy, sounds of laughter, gifts, and prayers. And more milestones follow, each with careful thought given to the treasure of life, from birth throughout maturation. From the iconic first birthday to those celebrated at ages five, sixteen, and twenty-one, we gather and celebrate. Then we move past age milestones to those based upon accomplishments instead of years of life. First jobs, graduations, marriage, children, professional accomplishments, retirement—all these seem to mark our way, complete with advice from those who have gone before us. Then maturity brings a critical shift in our season of life. We confront our mortality. Planning is now geared to future essentials, to leaving resources and a legacy for those we love.

Before, we celebrated milestones of life, but now, as the end approaches, we fall back on traditions that structure the milestones of death. Time begins to advance its pace. Life in its beginning brings tears of joy, but new tears come as we say goodbye to those we love. The gender reveal party is replaced with hospice, memorials, and gatherings of mourners. "For what is your life? It is even a vapor that appeareth for a little time, then vanishes away" (James 4:14 KJV).

Sorrow is to humanity as oceans are to whales. You cannot have life without sorrow; neither can a whale live without an ocean. Sorrow, like death, is part of life. The concept of death is neither conceptually inviting nor contextually understood. This writing will bring clarity to your purpose in the midst of suffering and death—to the greater value you can find while facing life-altering events. Many talented and gifted individuals have surrendered or allowed their dreams to expire while processing events that bring sorrow or death. After we experience a death—whether of a person or of a dream—we may look up and ask, *What is the true value and meaning of life's milestones?* Then we may ask, *What now? Where have all the milestones gone? What do we have to hold on to? Where have the gatherings, the celebrants, the mourners gone?* If we face the wake of mortality, if we stop making progress, if we stall or stagnate, we often don't know how to advance. To advance, one must face mortality or face one's loss. Denial is a form of stagnation; it impedes progress, interrupts purpose, and gives way to complacency. Let's trade complacency for *after*; life is full of endless possibilities.

Our old milestones were like rungs of a ladder, leading us on to the next stage of life. But after life-altering events, what ladder do we now have to cling to?

"Man that is born of a woman is of few days and full of trouble" (Job 14:1). And mortality is inevitable for everything that lives. I went from newlywed to widower in nineteen months, and my shih tzu named Monday, "man's best friend," died shortly thereafter. Yes, the deaths of pets and humans, along with other deaths, will impact our lives. Wherever it shows its face, mortality breeds pain, tears, and feelings of grief, followed by unstructured conversations seeking to process a loss of this treasure called life. How do we face the future? *After* seeks to provide rungs to hold on to—to address a sound method to regain focus, establish direction, and move forward following a confrontation with mortality, in all its forms. And it does visit us in many forms. My mother's passing was sorrowful, but countless numbers of business leaders, ministry workers, pastors, husbands, wives, young adults, and communities are experiencing death in many areas of their lives without an obituary. The death of a dream, divorce, an unscheduled closing of a business, loss of a home, or continued struggle against prevailing pressures can affect us just as powerfully. The resulting sorrow can define the course of our lives. But if it is not harnessed and addressed, we cannot find *after*. When I faced these voids myself, I found a need for a guide to do just that, as it was impossible to find adequate support in a very dark season of life. That's what this book is all about. We must partner as believers and become sensitized, creating adequate support systems without discrimination.

If you are facing mortality that isn't physical, know that you don't have to accept the death notice on your life. You can refuse to give up the ghost. You can push the reset button. Resetting your life after sorrow is not only possible but critical. Just as you reset your computer or iPhone to eliminate bad data or corrupt files, determination resets your life. But beware: a reset or power down will not work should you fail to install the latest software updates. We must update your life's software—your way of thinking—as well. Old data will affect our ability to process life's desire for purpose or peace. My iPhone's capacity is massive, but the open windows from previous searches began to slow it down. My brilliant nine-year-old namesake grandson gave me instructions to clear the old. "Papi, go to the home button, hold it down, and push delete."

Complacency stems from outdated software in life; it destroys creativity and future opportunities. Your *after* will require resetting key concepts, allowing you to begin to see failure as a need to proceed while other choose to surrender and begin accepting a premature death. This breeds inspiration for champions. Disappointments are not fatal; they give light to value and will identify waste. And stagnation is not the end of the story; it can be a turning point to a new *after*. *After* says that even though you've faced pain, sorrow, and weighty burdens, a season of recovery is forthcoming. Let's embrace the future by deleting our past. Some believe forgetting is impossible, but forgetting is an invitation to trade bitter for better.

Facing Historic Sorrow

I was three years old when my biological father transitioned from this life. My memories of Andrew Carnegie Turner are not just cloudy; they are absent, short of pictures or stories. I could not display sorrow at his passing because a small child is ill-equipped to process death. My father passed in an era when natural causes were commonplace. I was three years old and very sick when Dad passed. In addition to rickets, scarlet fever and kidney failure added to my sickness. He was sick with scarlet fever, kidney failure, and other ailments when he died. My elder siblings displayed their sorrowful emotions when Dad passed. Sorrow waited three plus decades, then it found me without warning. I was married, had two daughters, was walking into successful goals of life—that's when my sorrow over Dad's mortality became visible. I share my dad's name but lacked capacity to understand his death until later in life.

Postponed sorrow is real, and denial often delays one's ability to reach *after*. The impact of my father's death finally reached me while I was sitting in one of my corporate offices. This sorrow waited until I became president and CEO of my engineering support services firm.

Andrew Carnegie Turner's presence appeared, to my unbelief, with a voice of approval, suggesting he had never left, although he was absent. He appeared in what psychologists call "present absence," when we come face-to-face with an unmet need. I witnessed his presence conceptually, while understanding Dad was unable to be physically present. Dad's presence in that moment created yet another sorrow; it was rewarding but painful. Suddenly, I had to address the huge hole within my heart. How does an adult miss or desire something or someone that has been removed from their community? The question has inspired many interpretations, causing us to examine our thoughts, inner desires, and longing for love. Humanity is created to embrace life and love; death will have a significant impact on our subconscious.

After is not just for those facing recent loss. It is for those who carry historic losses within them. It may be the loss of a parent, a family member, or a loss of hope brought on by circumstances beyond your control. It may be smaller losses piled one on the other, until one day you look up and realize that they have stolen your vital energy, effectively stopping your life. But we can prevail over historic mortality in much the same way we face immediate death: we make the decision to choose life. We use the loss to discover inner strength. And we walk forward with determination, rather than avoidance. Though it may be emotionally or tangibly costly, we make the decision to carry on.

Life must prevail over historic losses. Mortality must never defeat life metaphorically. Discover your inner strength through meditation and dedication to life. Walk forward with determination and avoid prolonged periods of self-incrimination. Vilification promotes periods of bondage. The emotional investment is far less rewarding than making a decision to carry on with life.

Historic losses may arise unannounced in your mind, causing confusion or perplexed thoughts. Life's historic moments seldom have expiration dates. Visitations such as I experienced with my deceased father are not uncommon; far from anything demonic, it's actually life visiting history. This loss was significant, and facing it was valuable. When it happened, historically, it had little impact, but dad's post-departure impact is both undeniable and real. Visiting the past is critical, but living in the past promotes unwanted trauma and causes us to miss new opportunities. Face it, and find help if needed; your *after* will become marginalized until history is resolved.

Invest in Life

Is there life after death? What cost must we pay to carry on? Everything in life is costly, including the decision to live. There might be a monetary cost, such as counseling or therapy, which is often a helpful aide to defining emotional temperaments. But how do we monetize the true value of counseling or therapy, knowing it helps define matters of life, sorrow, and death? This is controversial; some consider it vilifying sorrow, making it an extremely unacceptable means of support. Regardless of your resources, life must be seen as your priceless and timeless investment. You can decide today that it is worth the investment.

In life you will face a series of good and bad events; some are called successes while others seem dismal failures. *After* is the process of weighing both, failures and successes. You must decide, after this process, to change your expectations, even while others highlight your failures. Failure is never final until one decides death is acceptable. Failures are life's assets; they increase one's value, worth, and wisdom. I recall losing a political race with a sense of failure and declaring it would be the end of my time in public service and nonprofit positions. I later learned the dismal loss was actually necessary, for we seldom appreciate success without having lost a race. Losing an event does not make one a lifelong loser. Champions never allow a loss to predetermine their future. Winning is not everything, but it's priceless after experiencing a lost. The value of one who returns after a loss is greater than one who leaves because of a loss. In this book, you will continually be asked to decide to invest in life and to consider your losses as gains. Though struggles may seem overwhelming, though failures may seem final, and though complacency and stagnation may seem like the only viable option, I assure you—*after* is coming, and your investment will pay off. You will reach new milestones, and while the process may be arduous, they remain critically important. With time, effort, and determination, you will be able to lay hold of a brighter future, step by step, deposit by deposit. Decide today that you have what it takes to pay the cost in determination and to rise up after failure. You will find strength and comfort along the way.

A Comfort to Those Who Mourn

A phone began ringing before dawn. As I reached for it in the darkness, my fear became reality. On the other end of the line I heard my sister's labored breathing as she announced our mother had transitioned from this life. Death had made his call on the most amazing, loving, kind, stern, argumentative, strong-willed, caring mother in the world. Mother, affectionately called "Red Lady," was more than our biological caretaker. She had divine ethics, purpose, and great impartation. Through her decades of life, her voice gave wisdom, direction, prayers, and rebukes that molded and guided us. How could her life be over?

My youngest sibling simply announced: "Mommy is gone." Even now, four years after her passing, the memory brings tears to my eyes. Though I do not know when or if the pain of her passing will fade, I can find comfort by reflecting upon her immense contributions. Mother's contributions to life are remarkable. While she could not remember if she finished high school, she owned property, leased apartments, built remarkable fiscal habits, and maintained excellent credit, all while never owning a vehicle. Mother took her driving test in her mid-fifties then declared she would not drive while her husband was alive. Mother raised three blended families, giving equal love and attention without discrimination. She lived her last years in constant pain from arthritis and other complications. When we asked her how often she was in pain, she said, "Daily—there's not one day when my body is not hurting." But Mother's inspiration and determination continuously overshadowed her personal pain.

Mother's death pained her surviving family members and countless friends, but we found solace knowing that her daily pain ended. Mother made valuable contributions, and her love lingers well beyond her memorial service. Her death brought tears, but along with it love and cherished moments of comfort.

A vital question remains: who or what comforts us while processing nonbiological "deaths"? How do we mourn a bankruptcy? No one meets a failed marriage or ministry with a great reveal celebration or a heartfelt memorial service. A divorce decree ends one season but another begins immediately after, affecting family, children, business, and finances. *After* explores death in concept, and it seeks to bring life to this mental mortality. It seeks to answer the questions like the ones I've faced in life: What happens when your business fails? Can you survive the public scrutiny and opinions surrounding a ministry that must file bankruptcy? What are the impacts of divorce upon your life and business? What hole shall become your residence during this adverse season of life? Questions come rapidly without answers, and the temptation to cry failure is commonplace. How can you tell others to continue when your business partner violates ethical standards, bringing your dream to ruins? Who understands when your bride of two weeks announces she has stage-four cancer and she will transition from this life within nineteen months of marriage? How do you enjoy a honeymoon when chemotherapy starts forty-eight hours after the elaborate wedding ceremony? Questions like these are often met with painful silence, but *after* speaks directly to them in simple, practical terms. And just as my family found comfort in the fact that our mother is now experiencing life after death, we can find comfort that there is life *after* our personal setbacks too.

Society restricts or frowns upon mourning. Physical or mental expressions of mourning are forbidden in some cultures. Grief, if not managed, alters daily routines of life, making simple tasks seem impossible—and that's why others offer condolences, comfort, trays of food, quiet company, and helping hands. Death will affect our ability to deal with everyday life, even down to the smallest daily tasks. Such is the period of mourning.

I experienced this exponentially in the months surrounding my mother's passing. Death continued to call, taking loved one after loved one. My wife's death preceded mother's passing, as an aggressive form of cancer shortened her life at forty-two years young. Within months my elder brother and another friend would pass in quick succession. Les, my board member and riding partner, would also transition three months thereafter. Death made eight consecutive visits without ceasing.

Unconsciously these occurrences created a dark season in my life. It became simply unmanageable; I had become dead to life. To find my *after*, I had to accept another painful truth: life will be altered by unmanageable deaths or external events. The unmanageable events will affect everything about your daily existence in the period of mourning: your processing capacity, your ability to manage sleep, your eating habits, and the way you seek solace in other places, only to find more sorrow than joy. These unmanageable moments do not signify weakness, for it takes courage and strength to continue while facing one or more visits of death.

Of course the effects are real and sometimes lasting. But strength comes in realizing that life does exist after death, because *after* comes to those who have obtained new courage and fortitude to live again.

Total restoration is never achieved without change and loss. I recently asked Siri how to restore a home. She said it had to be stripped to the frames or beams to expose the most critical elements. Plumbing, electrical conduits, and insulation to keep heat in and cold out must be exposed prior to restoration. Writing *After* was impossible without experiencing multiple losses. Life seems to rise to new heights following a stripping. A refurbished home is worth more than its predecessor. That's true in your life; your value increases during the advancement after a loss. You are equipped to provide authentic value to life, so get up and give.

Perhaps the greatest comfort I can offer to those who mourn losses of all kinds is that *after* is a choice, and you can make it even when faced with unmanageable events, even if it seems that everything has been taken from you. It may require periods of rest and mourning, but it begins as a mind-set—an internal determination. It can be as simple as saying to yourself, *My life must carry on, and I will choose life over death.*

After goes beyond material loss. It urges you to discover your core value to find inspiration to lift life from your ruins.

In the coming chapters, we will determine maneuvers with clear, concise objectives geared toward a new and greater you. We will focus on "forgetting what is behind," using Paul's words as inspiration to leave that dark place so we can look toward the future (1 Corinthians 3:13). We will explore the effects of sorrow, how to become shatter resistant, how to take time to heal and leave isolation, and how to push beyond history. Then, having spoken to your darkest place in life, you will be encouraged to find an authentic *after*, and find direction and encouragement for a better quality of life.

Perhaps for you, sorrow has lingered long beyond its season. Sorrow has a new opponent, and it is called life. *After* is your new mind-set; it will replace sorrow, producing renewed hope combined with vigor and vitality. Just as we find structure in life's celebrations, milestones, and memorials, you will find your momentum again as you walk slowly forward toward your *after*.

Reflection Questions

1. How has sorrow been an opponent in your life? What would it look like to face that opponent head on?

    _____

    _____

    _____

2. In what area of life are you seeking *after*? How can drawing a line between *before* and *after* help you build a renewed mind-set?

    _____

    _____

    _____

3. Have the costs of investing in life ever seemed too high? What does it mean to you to be prepared to pay those costs?

    _____

    _____

    _____

4. Following a loss, death, or long period of stagnation, how has the process of mourning affected your everyday life? How is the concept of *after* a comfort in your mourning?

    _____

    _____

    _____

5. What does it mean to you to choose life over death in the areas of mortality you are facing?

_____

_____

_____

6. How have milestones provided comfort and structure in your life? How does knowing that milestones exist to lead you to *after* change your outlook on your situation?

_____

_____

_____

7. In what ways do you long to push the reset button on your life? Knowing the realities you face, how can pushing the reset button on your outlook change your view of failures, setbacks, and challenges?

_____

_____

_____

_____

CHAPTER 2

Shatter Resistant

*My brethren, count it all joy when ye fall
into diverse temptations.*
James 1:2 KJV

A piece of fine crystal stemware and a mason jar might hold your drink one just as well as the other, but they are unquestionably different in nature. Crystal is very costly and delicate; it comes in a set and used sparingly. A mason jar is rugged, bold, and thick; it's very durable and frequently used in casual situations. Crystal shatters on impact. A mason jar, unlike crystal, can withstand repeated impacts and not shatter.

When it comes to your *after,* you can choose to be more like a mason jar, experiencing impacts and multiple disappointments, without shattering. A shattered moment may occur while in pursuit of dreams or purpose. It's never planned for, and much like shattered crystal it seems impossible to repair. Shattered crystal must be removed quickly to avoid cuts. In the same way, we must confront and move beyond shattered moments in our life to reach *after.* We must avoid stagnating, ruminating, overanalyzing, and losing our way in life. Though we may have shattered, we must sweep up the remains of our stemware and reach for a sturdier vessel, able to withstand impact in the future.

Shattering events usually affect family, faith, and finances, and place weights upon your future. Shattering moments are internal test of character or determination. Do not give up on life when this occurs. Every successful life began with some disappointment. Thomas Edison experienced three thousand failures before perfecting one light bulb. Picking back up in life is never easy, but living with lifelong regrets is unacceptable in your *after*. Dedication, hard work, and commitment will produce light in darkness. Shattering moments define periods of life, ordered by our Creator; they are designed to prepare His chosen believers for greater. Meeting a test is never comfortable, and failure is imminent where preparation or study is absent. We never know when we will meet or engage in "life testing," or the unscheduled, undesired element that seemingly has little or no value in life. In our *after* we discover the value of that testing.

I discovered it during my work with Saint Jude Children's Research Hospital. I came to understand the heartbeat of that institution; they operate with an embrace, dedication, and commitment to serve the loving, innocent children who are undergoing extensive treatments for cancer. When did I gain this appreciation, and why does this commitment remain while others have evaporated? I was called to care for cancer patients, namely children, while experiencing the final transition of a spouse who suffered violently from liver and pancreatic cancer. I rose up empty, feeling shattered, but purpose was birthed out of my loss and inability to find support while facing this dark hour. Help for others emerged from the darkness.

Withstanding a Shattering Blow

March 2008 began like each preceding month of that trying year. This was the year when economic instability gained momentum, bringing pain and suffering to countless communities. Home foreclosures became commonplace in 2008, and major corporations began

failing. General Motors stopped producing many of its previous flag-
ship models, while banks continued to profit from bankruptcy filings.
The American dream had turned into a nightmare on Elm Street.
Wall Street placed blame on Congress, real estate developers blamed
the banks, and some blamed each other as their life savings and their
American dreams faded in fiscal misery.

Epic levels of pain and suffering occurred in 2008 in a shattering
moment across our society. Some gained inventory at the expense of
others' losses. Thousands lost their savings and hope for the future
with one foreclosure letter. Detroit, Michigan, and other iconic man-
ufacturing cities ground to a halt, leaving whole communities in
desolate conditions.

How do we withstand such shattering blows? What do we do
when faced with desolate conditions? Perhaps the simplest place
to start is the closest to the heart: prayer. Never underestimate the
true value of a divine relationship in desolate times. An established,
ongoing relationship with God may not remove a crisis, but your
chances of survival are increased exponentially while in the crisis.
You'll reach *after* through dedicated personal inspirational development, including prayer and meditation.

It's easy to forget the importance of prayer in times of plenty.
But your *after* is a spiritual move first and foremost, and you become
more resilient, more attuned to God's leading and will for your life
through prayer.

I began an unusual prayer vigil in my congregation mid-2008.
The economic crisis was widespread; churches were losing members, members were losing employment and homes, students were
leaving college, and foreclosures by predatory lending institutions
were escalating.

Our simple prayer was for strength, guidance, and comfort. No
one thought of surrendering; no, we asked the Father for vigor, insight,
and rest. No one sought to rise up while celebrating another's down-
fall. We gathered every Monday for two consecutive years asking
God for the simple treasures of life—strength to endure, light to lead

us through darkness, and comfort for longer-than-understandable nights. *Our Father, which art in heaven, hallowed be thy name ...*

Prayer Closet was held every Monday during NFL season. Hundreds gathered each week for three consecutive years, understanding prayer was exceeding the value of Monday Night Football. "But thou, when thou prayest, enter into thy closet, and when thou hast shut thy door, pray to thy Father which is in secret; and thy Father which seeth in secret shall reward thee openly" (Matthew 6:6). This is the simple value of prayer.

Survival Mode

My life, like many others' in 2008, was moderately trying as financial matters began to affect daily routines and savings began to dwindle. My objective was clear: *Don't complain, remain grateful, and you will live through this season.* Then March 2008 delivered a life-shattering blow unlike previous financial challenges. Life can move from trying to epic survival mode instantaneously.

I became partially paralyzed in March 2008 due to an unforeseen disk compression that blocked the flow of spinal fluids. The loss of mobility was earth-shattering, and it required immediate high-risk surgery. I was not prepared to accept this shattering condition as it aggressively overtook my motor skills.

My prognosis was unfavorable. Several neurologists deemed my condition inoperable, citing possible negative outcomes including permanent paralysis and loss of speech. With every negative report, I had to determine how to react: would I shatter, or would I keep living, no matter the circumstances?

Our mental aptitude is often challenged by external circumstance. The mind operates in multiple-choice algorithms. A brain has in excess of billions of cells, capable of developing hope, failures, fears, thoughts of joy, and feelings of failure. When we are unsure of how to carry on, we often make decisions as students do in a multiple-choice test, blindly choosing a path forward and hoping for the best. How often have you made a decision knowing it was not necessarily the right one? How often have we avoided wisdom for comfort or sought an easy solution to a complex problem? Time is valuable; use it wisely to make wise decision, knowing that in your *after* you are equipped or prepared for the testing. *After* gives us the freedom of choice to accept defeat or become a "more than conqueror" in Him who loved us (Romans 8:37). Paul is extremely insightful in Romans 8 because he sees the value of maintaining strong commitment to Christ through various personal affronts. Shattered individuals don't fight; they surrender. Individuals seeking *after* will sweep away the broken pieces and continue with life.

Two alternatives exist when conditions shatter the infrastructure of your life, business, ministry, or family. The first option, defeat, is unacceptable because failure requires quitting. Our second option is to pursue success in the midst of adversity. This will require purpose, dedication, patience, a plan, and support.

Better from Losses

When the Golden State Warriors played the Cleveland Cavaliers for the 2017 NBA championship, both teams entered this final series knowing one would obtain the title and ring while the other would become second best. Players never train to lose, but losing is often a prerequisite to winning. To appreciate winning you must learn how to recover from a loss. It means acquiring inner strength to remain a professional athlete while the opposing team accepts the trophy.

In professional sports, only one team will become a champion per season. But there can be innumerable champions in life. Each of us is a professional dreamer; we are people with vision, character, and purpose. Our championship ring is won by possessing daily confidence. Some have never realized success until after a bout with defeat. Never allow shattered moments, relationships, dreams, or health to diminish your purpose or value. Remember the mason jar; it's bold, strong, and durable.

How do we learn to lose like a champion? To not only survive in shattering circumstances, but carry on to a greater future? By doing what the professionals do. They process the pain, keep moving, and grow in the face of opposition.

Process the Pain

Certain events in life produce painful memories, and others pass quickly. We can't deny the pain of a loss, but ultimately, we come to a point where we must choose to hang on to that painful event or move past it. The question is, how long will the pain last? Onlookers might question your strength as a man or woman based upon your processing timetable. How long is long enough to grieve the loss of a loved one? Should pain subside with a divorce decree? It does not end there! Small business failures occur daily; many ventures never succeed beyond five years of service. Does the business owner close when there's no business, or when there's no option but death? Divorce rates have climbed to astounding levels and even higher for second marriages. Ministers or pastors are leaving pulpits in record numbers, and according to studies 150,000 parishioners leave their local church each week.[1] These forms of death produce pain and mourning, and we all react in different ways.

Pain has its own language. And to find *after,* we must learn to understand that language—and how to speak and reply. Pain, unlike French, Spanish, or German, is universally understood. Tears in German, French, or Spanish symbolize one is undergoing pain or sorrow. Silence is part of the language of sorrow. Sleep deprivation, overeating, depression, outbursts, and emotional breakdowns are part of this language. The grammar of pain includes behavior changes, mood swings, or a move toward more extreme introversion. Pain will alter our lives until a healing occurs; and healing comes through understanding and reacting to pain in wise and intelligible ways.

When we face pain, we can reply in two different ways: with bitterness or enhanced passion. Passion has value; it creates new opportunities when channeled into positive measures of life; it creates better lemonade than bitterness. Bitterness stifles a life; it creates sickness, weakens health, and contributes to untimely deaths. Bitterness is a form of shattering due to a painful event. Developing passion through the pain, on the other hand, is a form of bouncing back—getting back in the game.

After a loss, we cannot deny that it happened, and we cannot stop the pain. But we can control how we react and learn from the pain.

Keep Moving

Ultimately, losses of material objects, business operations, marriages, or ministries are exceptionally painful, but never fatal. Time is a finite unit, so wasting years or months asking, "How did this happen?" is counterproductive. The ability to *move* brings us into recovery mode. The mobility of our lives begins with clear decisions. We make a plan to move forward. Some believe the absence of a precise plan is failure. But in the face of a shattered moment, the lack of movement is a plan for failure.

I was a senior planning engineer for Lockheed Martin; this required developing strategic, programmatic measures to accomplish critical software tests and evaluations, leading into system deployment. The risk-mitigation process required coming up with in-depth alternatives called "what-ifs." This knowledge became valuable, allowing us to predict the impacts of delays, on-time deliveries, or integration of other elements. In short, a plan creates a pathway to success. Start planning and moving toward your recovery; it's a sure pathway to success.

While it can be beneficial to analyze what went wrong in some situations (we'll address this in a later chapter), some people spend years asking rhetorical questions regarding a business failure or unfortunate incident in life. Don't fall for this trap. My 2008 surgical procedure required an expedited decision. Waiting for the answer to "How did this happen?" was futile; we had to make the urgent decision to move into surgery. Remember the shattered crystal we discarded to make room for new? If you sit still and save the broken pieces or memories, if you draw them to yourself, continually picking them up and examining the shards, you'll cut yourself and lose valuable lifeblood. This practice of ruminating on what went wrong often delays or destroys new potential.

After gives support needed to regain momentum and find direction. Find options—many are available, but avoid choosing quick fixes. Move in this new direction by first identifying available options. And we must rule out what is not an option. Quitting, or remaining shattered, is no longer an acceptable option. *After* requires a resilient attitude complete with renewed courage to see future possibilities. Nothing will change until you begin to accept this challenge. Crystal is fragile and easily broken, but you are strong, vibrant, and resilient. You possess will, power, might, and durability. Crystal may shatter beyond repair, but our lives are priceless entities. We are often disappointed, dropped, and confused by extreme circumstances, yet we remain shatter resistant.

Shattering experiences are never easy to overcome, but you possess a unique quality and strength to reach *after* in this emotional moment. You can make the choice to keep moving—to reject rumination, stagnation, and defeat, and refuse to continue to harm yourself with the shards of your past.

Grow in the Face of Opposition

Thomas Rainer often says, "Leadership without opposition is impossible." The same is true in life. Opposition is valuable while others consider it to be shattering—it highlights strength or other positive attributes. It is often hard to know how to respond. I learned the pain of opposition first-hand. Betrayal by one employee destroyed my multimillion-dollar business. In 2006, right before my mother's death, this employee disclosed our firm's pricing formulas to a known competitor. Closing a once-successful firm after nearly ten years within the Federal Aviation Administration was traumatic. To learn an insider sold information to undermine our business operations created severe emotional shattering, leaving a trail of mistrust and anger. Betrayal destroyed the livelihood of employees, interrupted salaries, voided retirement benefits, and left in its wake vacant offices and useless furniture. Once again, death had called; this event darkened my dreams, buried my heart's effort, and for a moment left me breathless, feeling violated. Leaving E & I Systems under these terms felt fatal, but not for long. Shattered moments create opportunities. *After* is a bold invitation to the complacent, broken, and shattered.

My emotional shattering produced wisdom; it stimulated my willingness to partner with others who, like myself, have experienced various forms of defeat but will not remain defeated. These partnerships took on various forms, inside and outside of business. Forming new relationships is healthy and signals internal recovery, or a willingness to trust others. From these relationships and the strength gained during this experience, I now mentor several innovative leaders, male and female, and I began a new firm—not out of spite or to prove others wrong, but as a means to continue this life journey called *after*. Each negative experience in life has purpose, although it is often hard to find an immediate value following these events. *After* is the reward following an emotional shattering. Pain should sponsor passion and diminish fear.

After is a bold invitation to the complacent or broken but not shattered individual. This invitation requires momentum and the simple, daring decision to carry on. You know you will reach a point once again when you will see clearly how your shattering event has made you stronger. Climbing a mountain may seem foolish or risky until you reach its peak. Your field of vision on the peak of a mountain is far superior to that at its base. Getting to the top is never easy, but staying down impedes your view of many opportunities. Take the challenge, and climb this mountain called *after*. Collect the courage to move, and begin your ascent.

A Shatter-Resistant Generation

No matter your age or generation, you have likely come face-to-face with a shattering moment. But you can become resilient despite your challenges, shattering though they may be. *After* is a critical concept for all generations. Too many baby boomers are surrendering prematurely. A failed marriage, split ministry, sabotaged businesses, home foreclosures, health challenges, and general disappointments are simply knocks to our mason jars. We are stronger than crystal and able to take risks and a new journey into success.

Millennials and Generation Z also will face shattering moments from a different angle. Baby boomers know disappointment; we have lived through fiscal challenges, wars, divorce, divisiveness, and business failures. But for the younger generation, wealth of knowledge is escalating as commerce moves from production to creativity. Still, younger generations must prepare to meet inevitable setbacks and challenges. *After* is designed to give insight into life's coping skills, which are required to sustain your hard-won character following every new, inevitable disappointment. How will you rebound following your business downturn? Are you prepared to accept a loss for an extended period of time? What is your exit strategy? Asking these questions will enhance your strategy and preserve your momentum toward the future.

After seeks to reconfigure your mind-set both after and prior to disasters, deaths, and shattering moments—to provide concise principles and programmatic orders to produce a victorious journey. *After* is for those who have failed but are not failures. You are a sturdier vessel than you know, and you can grow to become shatter resistant.

Reflection Questions

1. Can you name a time when you have been more like crystal stemware than a mason jar? Have you cut yourself on old memories? How would you do things differently?

_____

_____

_____

2. What are the benefits of strengthening your prayer life and relationship with God before, during, and after shattering moments?

_____

_____

_____

3. Would you classify yourself as someone who knows how to lose well? How could losing well be a strength in your life?

_____

_____

_____

4. Has pain produced bitterness in any area of your life? How could you turn that pain into passion?

_____

_____

_____

5. How does accepting that quitting is not an option help you move after you've come to a standstill? In what ways do you need to move in a stagnant area of your life?

_____

_____

_____

6. In what ways do you face opposition in life? How might that create opportunity?

    _____

    _____

    _____

7. How do you see people in your generation coping with shattering moments? How can you embrace *after* as a generational movement?

    _____

    _____

    _____

CHAPTER 3

Healed While in Solitude

If you are just starting out on this journey to recovery, I applaud you. Emotional and spiritual recovery is seldom easy or quick. This process requires patience and endurance along with prayer, planning, and dedicated action. We often marginalize commitment and dedication, but these two simple attributes are critical to recovery after your shattering moment, and they are critical to restarting following a shattering or stagnation.

Commitment and dedication are most effective when healing occurs. To experience healing, we must embrace a healthy solitude. The key is, though, to not let healthy solitude become toxic by an overdose of sorrow while in isolation. In this chapter, we will discuss how to identify healthy isolation and avoid the potential negative outcomes of solitude. In the next chapter we will explore how to embrace positive attributes of solitude and leave isolation.

How have you experienced solitude? Solitude is often a by-product of living through a crisis. If it turns into continued isolation, though, and begins affecting other elements of life, it breeds adverse complacency. It leaves us susceptible to patterns of negative thoughts, behaviors, or unhealthy pain-altering alternatives. It leaves us immersed in sorrow. Death is unavoidable to mortal beings, but through Jesus, we have spiritual authority, power, and might to control sorrow (Matt 18:18–20). Mitigating sorrow is critical to one's recovery; binding or controlling sorrowful thoughts is essential to reaching *after*. Sorrow is a very complex issue; it can interrupt or postpone our acceptance of offers to recover. It makes us fearful and closed to the good things in our lives.

Again, there is a difference between healthy solitude and prolonged sorrowful isolation. In a healthy solitude, we find time for prayer and meditation. In prolonged isolation, we become cut off socially, prime targets for deeper social problems such as addiction, chronic loneliness, or an uptick of suicidal thoughts or considerations. In healthy solitude, we find purpose and inspiration, including thoughts of *after*. In isolation, we become distracted and neutralized by regrets. In a healthy solitude, we take time to reposition ourselves and release the things that hold us back. On your journey toward *after,* you can choose to reject the pitfalls of sorrowful isolation and take advantage of all the good things a time of healing solitude has to offer. We will explore some keys to healthy solitude on your way to your *after,* while identifying tools to avoid the descent into prolonged isolation.

Go Directly to Your Gate

Los Angeles Airport, like Dallas and Chicago O'Hare, is configured to lead passengers through complex traffic corridors before reaching their departure gates. A straight line is the shortest distance between two points. Your departure gate, of course, is the furthest point from civilization and never in a straight line. Airports are designed to enhance commerce by leading passengers past food courts, boutiques, and expensive high-end designer shops. On your way to your destination, you must maneuver through complex terminals with singular focus. Many gates are closer than yours, but are their destinations acceptable? Finding direction following a shattered or stagnant experience is much like walking through LAX Airport. You must remain focused on your gate or be left behind. *After* seeks to guide each passenger through recovery, giving simple directions to your desired destination. Gates to avoid include isolation, weariness, and failure. Stay focused upon recovery, life, happiness, and determination. Though you may take the walk alone, you can do it with purpose, knowing that you are walking toward a better place.

Walk Past Loneliness to Find Solace in Solitude

Loneliness and solitude might seem similar, but they are fundamentally different. Loneliness breeds depression and wayward thoughts. Solitude should become purposeful following a death or where shattered emotions exist, causing prolonged challenges. I have witnessed professional, accomplished men and women fall from productive lives into wayward behaviors because of loneliness.

What is loneliness? Webster's dictionary defines it as "a state of dejection or grief *caused by* the condition of being alone." Note that it is grief *caused by* being alone, and it is not the state of being alone itself. It is a pitfall to be avoided. The dejection of loneliness can have a critical impact upon one's life. One of my associates, an anti-trust lawyer, became lonely despite his prestigious accomplishments, and that loneliness sadly led him to attempted suicide in our corporate office. His value of life was tied to his loneliness. He was accomplished, young, brilliant, engaged to a wonderful attorney, and had a great salary, but he was lonely. Without hope or connection, he became a product of unhealthy loneliness. He became hopeless in the face of success. We must value hope and never stagger at the promises of hope.

To find your *after,* you must walk past loneliness and seek trustful relationships.

While you might need a period of solace or healthy solitude, make a point to remain connected to those you trust and love. Find trusting relationships instead of maintaining "situationships." Situationships are costly and reduce trust because, unlike in relationships, there's no accountability. Trust begins with defined commitments or bilateral agreements. Both parties in a trusting relationship must agree on core values that make the relationship safe and fruitful; situationships exclude core values of universal respect for each other. Clearly state what is needed from the friendship and obtain a commitment to maintain respected objectives while in recovery.

On a more positive note, simple words of appreciation can remind others that you want to remain a part of their lives, even while you heal and seek time alone to rebuild. The need for emotional support and words of wisdom may not come from one individual or resource. The need for company while watching a movie is far different than a voice of wisdom while sitting in a dark room. Knowing the difference is critical when pursuing *after*.

On the way to your destination, *after,* you walk past the gate of loneliness by making simple choices and taking simple actions to remained focused.

Walk Past Regret to Find Your Future

Some gates in an airport are close to TSA checkpoints, but seldom will your flight depart from gate A1. No, it's in terminal C, gate Z65. Walking through terminals A and B, en route to terminal C, there's a temptation to observe others in these areas patiently waiting for their departure. There are planes in each gate, yet only one has been assigned to your destination. Temptation is the presence of easy alternatives; avoid these distractions. And one of the greatest temptations in our aloneness is to succumb to regret. Greatness bypasses failures and reaches for success. Regrets should not hold progress hostage.

When we spend a great deal of time alone, regrets tend to surface. As we ruminate, they can become overwhelming. In your healthy solitude you can choose to handle regret rather than succumbing to it. We all have an infinite number of regrets in our lives, whether they are public failures or private choices. But we must choose not to allow them to define our *after*.

Regrets are emotional events seeking to prohibit our purpose or mobility. If the event produces wisdom and not bitterness, it becomes valuable. If we can learn from our regrets, they become life-giving, not life-taking. Place wisdom into your carry-on. If regrets bring sorrow and tears, they're toxic to this season of life. Do not carry toxic waste on this journey; it kills wisdom. Travel light and wise!

Regrets can become assets to life and contributions to wisdom. Examine regrets with an eye for wisdom, seeking to become one who avoids relapse. Our lives are purposeful while shrouded in pain and dark experience. While regret can marginalize your power and take your vitality for life, passion and wisdom are its antidotes. The regret of a failed marriage is beyond comprehension—until you find love and become wiser, stronger, and more vibrant. Divorce is terminal A, gate 1. Love is terminal C, gate Z65. Keep walking past regrets until you reach the gift of love.

Sitting down at the gate of regret will not take you where you want to go. In your solitude and quiet moments, use your strength and mind to eliminate toxic thoughts and retain only that which provides wisdom.

Walk Past Hopelessness and Find Restoration

My two loving daughters have both wrecked vehicles beyond repair. Thankfully they were both well and unharmed after these accidents, but each vehicle was totaled, deemed unusable. As their father, I wanted to inspect both vehicles, only to be told they had been moved and placed for recycling. Because the cars were beyond hope, I had to let them go. Then settlement checks came from the insurance company, erasing my need to observe the debris. We could focus on finding new cars for them to drive. In a similar way, *after* settles our losses with hope and removes debris.

Hope writes us a check for the future. Restoration is of no effect when hope is absent, when we insist on examining and hauling around the wreckage rather than accepting the check and moving on. Picking up a broken life is impossible when hope is absent. Restoration follows hope, as it was with Abraham, who "against hope believed in hope" (Romans 4:18). Abraham hoped against hope to receive Isaac, a son conceived in his old age. Hope is often acquired while in solitude. Embrace hope knowing eventually your departure gate and desired destination shall come to reality. Hope is believing that God is bringing all things together for our good (Romans 8:28).

Hopelessness leads to compromise or finding an alternate means to reach *after*. The temptation to compromise is often great when we face unwanted delays. But embrace hope instead of compromise. Hope speaks to the future while in a storm. Hope speaks of healing during chemotherapy. Hope finds gate Z65 after a long, lonely walk through alternative gates. Hope is the most important item in your carry-on.

Carry-on restrictions limit the content, size, and weight of our luggage. Some of us are dragging around events that weigh us down, leaving us unable to board flights to success, victory, or recovery. Walk to your gate with hope, along with divine inspirational thoughts. In your times of solitude, embrace the hope given to us by God. It will give you permission to sort through that luggage and discard what cannot be used. Hope is most effective when you release toxic contents, weighty issues of life, and dark memories of your past. David's simple prayer works: "Create in me a clean heart, O God, and renew a right spirit within me" (Psalm 51:10 ESV). To find hope, call out to God and depend on Him. He brings us a future and hope (Jeremiah 29:11).

Hope itself, however, will never lighten our baggage. We must let it energize us to take action and remove heavy or potentially hazardous hopelessness before undertaking this trip to *after*. Hope becomes transformative by leaving weighty historic elements and seeking bountiful blessings.

Walk Past Unforgiveness to Find Freedom

When we are alone, our memories often recall the times we were wronged. Thus comes the pitfall of unforgiveness. Memory is traumatic when it produces unforgiveness. Giving enormous attention to others' critical, painful actions gives way to prolonged sickness, anguish, or captivity. Unforgiveness is a form of self-incarceration.

No one willingly seeks imprisonment, knowing the stresses and hardships of confinement. Rehabilitation inside a prison is rare, if not impossible. So how do we gain freedom from the prison of unforgiveness? Scripture declares rehabilitation and freedom comes from Christ: "If the Son sets you free, you will be free indeed" (John 8:36 NIV). Unforgiveness breeds bitterness or physiological pressures. If someone has caused you pain, suffering, disappointments, death, hurt, or fiscal devastations, of course these sufferings are valid; yet, let's not remain imprisoned by these negativities. You may not have had a choice in the actions of another person, but you do have a choice in how you will respond. God has forgiven your sins, and He is the one who is the ultimate Judge. Justice belongs to Him (Hebrews 10:30).

So how are we to trust again after a violation or broken relationship? Separate facts from fiction, value from waste, and pray the prayer of forgiveness. What bride does not know the difference between a cubic zirconia and a diamond? Christ asked the Father to forgive us, stating "They know not what they do" (Luke 23:34). Apply this principle in your everyday life and relationships. Relationships, marriage, and ministry are vital to our God. And He calls us to love and forgiveness. In your time of solitude, continue to relinquish to Him any unforgiveness you might carry, and you will be freed from that prison. You will move past hurtful events, walking toward your destination unencumbered.

Walk Past Addiction to Find Healing Silence

Most traumatic events occur without warning. As I watched footage of Japan's record tsunami, I saw it destroy homes, airports, infrastructure, and life itself. There was little or no sound in the footage of this destruction other than occasional voices of amazement.

Silence heightens when we face shattering moments. Searching for understanding or reasoning is futile. Trust me; it's hard enough to breathe, let alone find words to express the emotions associated with shattering moments or cumulative pressures. We can choose to use this silence to resolve emotions, or we can internalize them. Sometimes addictions are birthed from internalizing unresolved shattered events. And we tend to gravitate toward numbing behaviors to deal with emotions we cannot express.

To my strong male counterparts, who tend to internalize rather than express, finding a safe place to rebuild is critical if not essential to avoid costly addictions. Also, even though women often find it easier to express emotions, leaving them continually unresolved can also lead to addictions or unwanted behaviors.

While we might be tempted to use moments of silence or even a drug to numb ourselves, we can also choose to use them for a recreational purposes or as an escape from the perils of life. This is today's definition of an addiction.

After is the process of rebuilding your life following your personal tsunami. We must never allow unplanned destructive moments in life, time, business, or finance to render us permanently paralyzed or develop a codependency upon alternative means of support.

Embrace Healthy Solitude

Rebuilding, reviving, and restoration are a part of a process, not a project with one singular goal. Our lives can be viewed through systematic processes. Give yourself permission to accept regrets, sorrows, and associated outcomes during that process. Now proceed to recovery with patience, leaving isolation but benefiting from silence.

Our prayer moments are most valuable in times of silence, because in the silence, He speaks. Offer Him thanksgiving, not only complaints and venting. Love God with your whole broken heart, and begin sharing with Him your true innermost feelings when you are alone. As a child, my life was full of hospital stays and adverse sickness, but comfort came through my mother's prayers and stability. I was too young to understand her silence in my room until she passed recently. Her death introduced me to the value of being silent until divine strength was granted.

Once we have walked past the destructive elements of being alone, we are free to seek restorative solitude. We purposefully embrace the many gifts that times of silence bring us: meditation, time to think, and refocusing. This is the time to sit at your desired gate, before your plane takes off, and collect yourself. Meditation is critical; it brings focus to confusion. It prepares you to move to a new destination. In this time, you will define your strengths, know your weaknesses, seek opportunities, and conqueror your threats.

When to Ask for Directions

Quiet moments are priceless: they reveal untapped resources, including recovery and internal fortitude. In times of quiet, you can also assess your capacity for recovery and take steps to obtain external help if needed. You will know the true value of help when it is sought and not offered. If you are without progress, this is a signal that it is time for external assistance. Push past pride and find advice or external help when it seems there is no way forward. Progress should be a natural sequence based upon desires, determination, and purpose; when it is not, do not fail to ask for help, as you would ask for directions in an international airport. You are an American unable to read French, and asking for help can make all the difference.

Reset and Reposition

As you walk by the pitfalls of isolation, sitting quietly to find direction, take the time you need, but know that the purpose of this time is to reset your life. This repositioning time says to take action and rejoin the world.

Repositioning a life or an organization is a critical process following a shattered moment. The process is much like traveling by several gates at the airport. Repositioning will often feel like an exhausting, endless task. But each gate will be followed by the next until you reach the designated gate Z65.

Some people spend years or decades poring over life without making a decision to move to the next gate or reposition themselves. Some spend a lifetime writing a journal and never live what was written. You must live by inspiration or die by procrastination. Repositioning starts with a mind, body, and soul reset. It is an internal decision to move forward.

I recall that in 2008, when others were losing real estate investments, jobs, retirements, and basic needs, my life was jolted with paralysis stemming from disk compressions. The pain and weakness lasted for what seemed like a lifetime. Morphine and other pain medications were like trying to feed the hungry without food. I was confined to a walker, could not use a pen or pencil, spoke with slurred speech, and lost all normalcy in my life. One of my doctors believed in my recovery, while others declared my life would be permanently altered with a need for constant care. That is when I hit the reset button in my mind. My mind began speaking life, while pain and muscle weakness boded ill for my future. You will find your *after* during these dark moments. Resetting is a choice to carry on. Repositioning is turning yourself to face in the right direction.

Hitting the reset button requires perseverance while knowing the results may be laborious and slow. Patience is required during this process. Resetting your life is vastly different than rebooting a computer or electrical circuit breaker. Our lives are not mechanically engineered to reset by flipping a switch. Regardless of your financial status, education, status, or culture you have access to internal resources through patience, perseverance, and choice of attitude. Broken men or women come in all forms, some in pulpits, others in corporate America, and others in everyday walks of life. *After* believes internal motivation is available to all; it is fuel for living with confidence while stagnation seeks to render one hopeless or desolate. Decide to reset your inner life and reposition yourself for success.

In times of quiet, our minds are often in protect mode, which slows down or eradicates the potential of making a move or decision. So often we desire recovery in one swift move. The reality is, destroying a dream is easy, while rebuilding a shattered dream is often tedious. So regroup in your times of aloneness, consciously walking past loneliness, regret, unforgiveness, addiction, hopelessness, and all the other pitfalls of this quiet time. Keep walking toward your gate, and eventually you will board and take off into your future.

Reflection Questions

1. In what ways have you found aloneness healing in the past? In what ways have you found it destructive?

    _____

    _____

    _____

2. What are some personal warning signs you have experienced that told you that you were slipping from a time of solitude into isolation?

    _____

    _____

    _____

3. Which trustworthy individuals can you pinpoint to help you during your time of recovery? How can you keep a connection with them while preserving your necessary alone time?

_____

_____

_____

4. What is your plan when confronted with regrets? How will you learn from them and pray through them?

_____

_____

_____

5. What is your plan when confronted with hopelessness? How will you push away the wreckage and embrace hope?

_____

_____

_____

6. What is your plan when confronted with unforgiveness? What will your prayer of forgiveness be?

_____

_____

_____

7. What addictive or numbing behaviors are you prone to turn to during isolated times? What is your plan to replace or turn away from them?

_____

_____

_____

8. What are you looking forward to most in your time of healthy solitude?

_____

_____

_____

CHAPTER 4

Leaving Isolation

A patient with an extremely dangerous virus is placed in isolation for two reasons: containment and healing. His world becomes increasingly small until a medical expert declares an abatement or antibody has contained this virus. The patient will remain in closed quarters until another medical expert declares that it's safe to leave isolation.

Chapter three addressed the pitfalls of isolation that comes from shattering or stagnating events in our lives. You may remember that solitude is different than isolation. Solitude creates a sense of silence and brings one to reflect upon values and circumstances of life with the intent of making *after* a new lifestyle. Isolation may come after a period of shock or grief, but it needs to be managed in order to avoid negative or prolonged outcomes.

In a quarantine situation, isolation is necessary to stem infectious disease and to sterilize an infected environment. Our emotional immune systems are often compromised during seasons of isolation, leaving us emotionally weak. Children, family members, neighbors, or associates may feel the byproduct of your shattering.

If our shattering event or situation is like a virus, *after* offers two alternatives, but both are critical. The recovery must begin with you then spread to others within your circle. Airlines use this principle on each flight: "Put your mask on first, then assist your children or those traveling with you."

Some forms of isolation might be seen as extreme, and others mild, but remain under care until your recovery from the shattered position is complete.

Intensive Care

What is the proper course of action when hardships occur in our lives?

Some emotional infections are severe and require an ICU, while others are minor and can be addressed with outpatient care. Regardless of your level of infection, care is essential for *after*, but the time required will vary. The death of a mother or loved one produces various levels of grief and will require care according to the level of that grief. Infectious moments appear after divorce, child abuse, incarceration, medical diagnosis, or financial bankruptcy. I know some peers who suffer burnout in ministry. Paul, in Ephesians 4:1, speaks of walking worthy of this vocation. Charles Spurgeon experienced "fainting fits" during his ministry tenure. This creates a broader issue for professionals, ministry leaders, or caretakers: where do they receive care? Who provides care to caretakers when they are fainting? We must not neglect it, but at the same time we cannot live in quarantine forever.

Prolonged isolation might give one a sense of safety from the storms of life, but it impedes our access to freedom; it bears down upon our creative mind, and if unchecked it will become an excuse leading us into fear. Isolation is often required when infectious diseases occur, but we must eventually leave this stage of life, seeking solitude, then freedom. *After* offers systematic recovery while others see isolation as failure.

The outcomes of prolonged isolation are similar to the pitfalls we discussed in chapter three.

They might include:

1. Unforgiveness

2. Bitterness

3. Complacency

4. Addiction

5. Anger

6. Physiological disorders

7. Mistrust

These are real struggles. Death and disappointments can cause prolonged moments of isolation or loneliness, followed by mistrust. This cycle is predictable, but we must break away if we are to reach our destiny or purpose. I know because I have experienced it myself.

My justification for isolation and loneliness had merit. Emotional and mental isolation seemed warranted when a business deal failed within weeks of memorializing both my mother and my wife. The absences of loved ones along with betrayal by a business partner seemed to justify becoming bitter, withdrawn, and isolated. Sleep deprivation followed, food became useless, and emotional irritations increased, producing deeper isolation.

Isolation became my active partner; it led to my becoming angry even with God because these experiences felt unfair. My desire for life declined rapidly and continued to spiral downward. Friends became associates, for they were ill-equipped to offer advice or support during this extreme shattering season. However, these shattered moments led me into this quest for *after*. I know there are others like me who have experienced death but have not recovered. Some remain isolated, others broken, bitter, or angry. But I assure you, there is hope for change. Though it may be difficult, we can take steps that will lead us out of quarantine and out of isolation. We begin by learning to trust.

Learning to Trust Again

Disappointments should not justify prolonged periods of isolation and loneliness. Trusting others for direction or assistance is normal, but abnormal circumstances often require highly qualified or trained individuals, such as advisors, counselors, doctors, and trusted experts. My circle of friends became immediately disqualified to extract me from my advanced state of shattering. None of my professional associates had experienced death to this degree—a business, mother, and wife within months. Most lacked experience with this magnitude of loss, so my isolation seemed increasingly justifiable. I remained extremely disappointed with my peers. I considered some associates cruel and careless relative to these extreme losses. Today, in my *after,* I realize empathy does not equal capacity. My associates or friends had great intentions, but most lacked the capacity to effect change. The severity of this season required skilled capacity. Sometimes we must seek and find assistance from a triage specialist, whether it is a counselor, coach, doctor, or advisor.

Our friends and associates may be empathetic without having skill or capacity to challenge isolation or loneliness. Knowing this truth would have prevented the growth of mistrust in my relationships. Mistrust is a byproduct of social deprivation.

Breaking mistrust is strenuous work both mentally and spiritually. Mistrust is one's internal fortress based upon previous encounters, disappointments, or general mishaps in life. Society may tell us we are justified in constructing walls and boundaries whenever inequities occur. While this may look like wisdom, true wisdom alters behavior without isolating the entire village. Those walls of mistrust will cause you to reject new beginnings, love relationships, business opportunities, or your *after.* Yes, we must tend to our emotional wounds and allow them to heal, but becoming completely isolated by mistrust is counterproductive.

How do we fight mistrust? I started this journey by learning to identify integrity in others. Mentoring in business, family, and ministry is a critical element of my life. In the past, however, I frequently sought to mentor those with a desire to learn while failing to evaluate their level of integrity. David possessed integrity while serving Saul. He never sought to undermine Saul, or destroy or kill Saul while serving. My engineering business partner was highly educated but lacked integrity. My associate minister was a great theologian but lacked integrity. Their less-than-integral behavior darkened my willingness to mentor and champion others for a season.

Rather than ceasing mentorship programs, I instead enhanced my skills to discern greed versus commitment, integrity versus intellect. I have resumed my passion for encouraging others without fear or mistrust. The joy of success outweighs mistrust.

A guarded, mistrusting posture often justifies placing limits on yourself and ceasing the activities that bring you joy. Life should become progressive and productive with growth, joy, peace, and internal happiness. In the face of mistrust we have two choices: remain isolated or imprisoned inside of your own world, or choose to end this prolonged period of quarantine by trusting others who have like desires for life. Follow your passion, not your pain. I encourage those seeking *after* to remember that passionate work produces intrinsic priceless rewards and connections with others.

To trust others, we must first acknowledge that our friends, associates, and loved ones cannot take away our pain. They cannot understand us perfectly. Only God can do that. And we may need to rely on qualified professionals to counsel us through our shattering times. But we must not allow others' limitations or imperfections to keep us disappointed and isolated. We are each members of the body, and though imperfect, we can each function together toward the common goal of new life in Christ (1 Corinthians 12). While one of us may need to be isolated for a time, like a limb in a cast or brace, we must not become fully disconnected from each other. Seek connections through your faith community, through your family, and through those God has put in your path. Maintain grace in this time as you learn to trust again.

Meditation

After loneliness and isolation run their course in life, healthy solitude is your *after* safe place. In it, you reap the benefits of moments
of meditation. In a conference I attended, Dr. Ronn Elmore, a PhD
in psychology, spoke on the value of meditation. Several prominent leaders listened attentively as Dr. Elmore expounded upon the
need for daily meditation to avoid thoughts of failure, mistrust, and
anguish, and how it keeps us from giving fear space within our lives.

Fear seeks to find space in our lives to destroy our passion. Fear
makes assumptions of what will happen before seeking to proceed.
Fear wants to invade our lives to create a false narrative by replacing power with weakness, confidence with insecurity, and desire
with lethargic behavior. Dr. Elmore contended that fear must first
receive an invitation, giving it access to our positive attributes.
Prolonged periods of depression, isolation, or feelings of victimization or rejection are invitations to fear. *After,* however, boldly rejects
fear. Scripture is replete with insight on how fear and life interact;
2 Timothy 1:7 tells us, "For God hath not given us the spirit of fear;
but of power, and of love, and of a sound mind."

After shares this value, emphasizing the need for meditation to
leave isolation and loneliness. According to Dr. Elmore, it's easy to
become extremely isolated or lonely as professionals. Professionals
maintain public images, policies, and procedures in systems that
leave no room for humanity or emotional shattering. Professionals
are expected to be immune to pain and sorrow. Consequently, they
fall into isolation and must live with extreme caution, with little
room for trust if they are going to maintain their position. Who is
able to hear a professional's shatterings and pain without endanger-
ing his public image? Where is help for professional men and women?
These are lawyers, doctors, pastors, bankers, and business owners.
Are they to remain in isolation as lonely individuals? Do they have
a right to be transferred out of quarantine?

Everyone, no matter their job or status in life, experiences
the pressures of maintaining the image they want to project. But

maintaining that image during a painful time can come with the high cost of isolation. The public scrutiny of professionals creates unique challenges knowing privacy remains paramount. Imagery during painful moments, if not resolved, beckons numerous unwanted outcomes or prolonged isolation.

To fight this, Dr. Elmore recommends a form of meditation that involves being in the world rather than by ourselves, and taking in what's around us with gratefulness. Meditation sees value in nature; it leads one from loneliness into solitude, or a place of peaceful thoughts. Meditation requires a payment of your time and nothing more. A walk or bike ride costs nothing except a decision to leave isolation each day until new experiences begin to replace painful memories. Meditation begins in silence and ends with thanksgiving. Listen to ocean waves or birds in nature while offering thanksgiving to God. You will find your point of view changed, and you begin to interact with the world again in a safe place.

I believe meditation should become a personal reflection with God and nature. This kind of meditation produces long-term healing and understanding that allows us to give help to others. Additionally, group Bible study, conferences, and walks in nature can present valuable opportunities for meditation.

Embracing Change and Helping Others

Isolation ends when we enter into another season of life. And progress never occurs without opposition. Our minds resist change, but change is necessary. Change happens through renewed minds. Paul clearly writes about this premise in Romans 12:1–2. The change is a direct link to transformation of your mind. Paul, or Saul, as he was known then, was blinded by a bright light which darkened his past views and gave revelation to a greater purpose. Change provides an opportunity to find a greater purpose.

Fear of failure and disappointment in marriage, ministry, life, or business can give rise to emotionally infectious conditions. As we've discussed, these conditions run their course, and we must leave isolation. I found God's voice to be remarkably clear following my season of isolation. He offered words of encouragement and allowed me to see experiences as tools to help others instead of excuses. Seek Him, and He will guide you out of your isolation and into usefulness again. Your desire to give life signals that isolation has run its course.

Leaving isolation was not easy for me, but *after* gave me cause to end this infectious period of my life. Helping others is a great alternative to living in isolation and loneliness. My wife's cancer, though it caused me unimaginable sadness, inspired me serve on the advisory council to Saint Jude Children's Research Hospital. Shatterings provide value when we help others. It's rewarding to participate in philanthropic endeavors instead of staying isolated or lonely. Find a cause—whether it is care for youth, supporting adult education, care for seniors, or care of animals. Leaving isolation will help free you from personal captivity. Every step out of it is another step closer to regaining life *after*.

Reflection Questions

1. In what situations have you felt the need for a "quarantine" in your life? Was it helpful or harmful?

    _____

    _____

    _____

2. What are the signals that it is time to leave quarantine?

    _____

    _____

    _____

3. What situations have caused you to mistrust others and build walls as a result? In what ways has mistrust kept you isolated?

    _____

    _____

    _____

4. In what ways can you begin to dismantle this mistrust? How can you grow from those hurts?

    _____

    _____

    _____

5. What joy-bringing activity can you reactivate to help connect you with others? What "passionate work" can you pursue?

    _____

    _____

    _____

6. In what ways can you work regular meditation, in nature or the company of others, into your daily life?

    _____

    _____

    _____

7. What cause will you champion as a result of your pain, and how will you participate in it in ways that bring you out of isolation?

    _____

    _____

CHAPTER 5

──── Pushing beyond History ────

Never allow history to define your purpose or *after.* We cannot escape our past history, but yesterday should not regulate our future.

Living in the past trades today's beauty for yesterday's memories. This kind of self-inflicted captivity is also self-defeating. Why live with historic pains, memories, or shatterings when life offers so much more? Living in the past defeats the joy of *after.*

If you've studied history, you know it is the study of past events relative to today's human affairs. We divide history into periods that govern the approach of study—for example, the Industrial Revolution or early American history. My history professor displayed apathy while teaching post-modern history. The content was marginalized because our professor had no passion for this subject matter. His delivery lacked enthusiasm and energy as he lectured on what seemed to us like irrelevant historic events. It prevented us from learning the valuable lessons this period had to offer. I would come to learn that the way we approach events of the past can determine how much we learn from them. If we give it too much or too little value, history can warp our present and future.

History, if valued, will provide insight and wisdom to your future. We should acquire value from the past, but not live in the past. History must be incorporated into the fabric of our lives, but it should not be our dwelling place. Think of it as seasoning, or salt. Salt has a place in homemade rolls, breads, cakes, and pies. Mother would often add "a pinch of salt" to her recipes, and the balance brought out the best in her sweet pastries. Without salt, they would not have tasted as good. But excessive use of salt in cooking will drastically alter the taste, making the food useless.

The study of our personal history is also essential to understanding the bygone days of our lives. Personal history may explain behavior or post-trauma responses to unpleasant memories. Finding *after,* our new present and future in life, requires us to seek to understand our history—but not to excess. Reflections of childhood experiences in the present should not become walls of bondage. A visit down memory lane is much different than packing your belongings and relocating to a permanent home on memory lane. Short mental visits are profitable; relocating into dark moments is unhealthy.

The shattering moments, deaths, or stagnation occurs in all of our lives. To find *after,* we must address history, knowing progress is often challenged or hampered by history. History establishes principles for life along with cultures, religious norms, and family structures, and it shapes how one processes life. We have varied responses to history. The end of war creates jubilation; conversely, a divorce decree provides marginalized jubilation combined with tears or heartbreak. Both are historic events with extremely different outcomes. An enriching, expansive life built on the lessons of history can be rewarding, offering endless potential. This place called *after* is attainable, and it offers new ideas and brighter days.

Walking into the Past

Life was not always challenging for me. At one point, my life felt complete, success was noticeable, and I had recently been elected Youth President of a mega international ministry while rising through the corporate ranks. Dr. James Nelson insisted that we travel to West Africa as a means to understand global disparity and cultural enlightenment. The impact of this trip would be immense. History books, the History Channel—nothing was akin to being in this place, a nation seemingly stuck in time. While beautiful, it was dangerous—hot but welcoming. This was a personal walk into history. It was redefining; this trip revealed purpose and rich culture, but it was also painful.

Nothing shared prior to arriving compared with the reality of this inequity of life. The trip reset my view of pain and has rewritten my definition of determination and strength. I traveled to West Africa, stepping back into history and seeking to gain insight to America's cultural inequities. Standing in a vacated slave portal, I heard stories of the pain, sufferings, and violent conditions within these walls.

While in West Africa, my suburban lifestyle suddenly became meaningless. One morning the hosting missionary insisted we visit the historic slave ports and give attention to lepers living in this area. Nothing he could say compared to the reality of this experience. The Smithsonian Museums, the King memorial, and Gettysburg seem like relics compared to this experience. Lepers lay in barrels without limbs, begging for alms, and the slave castles stood erect, suggesting death or time would never remove their benchmark in history. This horror in history created a deeper appreciation to remain relevant and real, and find an *after* no matter how long it took or the price to be paid.

We walked through narrow corridors into a small portal from which little or no air could escape, which produced death and suffering before slaves were sent to America for another level of captivity. I walked into the slave masters' courts and heard of their freedom with young females, only to throw them overboard if they became pregnant. A child-bearing slave had little cash value. This twelve-day journey expunged my previous thoughts of suffering or discomfort. I had to amend every thought of suffering after leaving this slave port.

History learned during this trip to West Africa has forever rewritten my appreciation and understanding of fortitude or strength.

I gained an awareness of life's cruelty and human determination. History gave me valuable insight without holding me captive. I was not a slave, but became sensitive to others' plights through history.

Unlike my old college professor, who devalued what he was teaching, I began to see the value history could offer, revealing the stories of life growing through pain. Nearly twenty years later, my life was once again transformed with history. Another trip, this time to Israel, revealed an overwhelming sense of history, from creation, Jewish law, temples, cultures, persecutions, and pain, to resilience and understanding Jesus the Christ. My historical journeys into Africa and Israel totally reshaped my perspective on the value of the past. Walking back into history was not an act of captivity or defeat. These two moments created enormous understanding and new commitment to character and resilience. In the face of history, we can learn a new perspective without translating past events into a lifelong crutch.

When it comes to your personal history, living with excessive memories or overactive lessons may cause emotional crippling. Life is short, and often our dim view of equity is darkened further through our limited experience. When I learned about adversities in West Africa and explored bomb shelters in Israel, it was as if I was looking through windows into extreme moments of suffering or persecution. But remarkably, children in West Africa played on steps previously used to usher men and women into slavery. Children in Jerusalem performed safety drills in case of bombing raids. I observed Jewish soldiers with automatic rifles on guard and in bomb silos as we toured the vast vineyards. Slave ports, bomb shelters—these inequities were key elements of enlightenment. My pseudo-perfect world was once again shattered as I witnessed life in these extreme situations.

Amid history, slave shipment, wars, and bombings, children have moved on and brought life and a future to places that could have stood for so much death. They play and grow, writing new history for these places.

We too can find new life even in the face of painful historic events. My own childhood history includes a battle with the illness rickets, which left me unable to walk until age three. This disease is obsolete today, but my entire life was changed by this sickness. While my history and formative years were marred by illness, yesterday's crippling moment has no impact on my walking ability today. In fact, it made me stronger and taught me fortitude.

We seldom reach security without a visit into history. *After* accepts history as moment in the past. History must not determine your future, but must bring value to your *after*.

Cultural History

Culture, according to Dr. Samuel Chand, shapes one's ability to process events or leave negative environments. Cultures are essentially unwritten systems inside our communities. Culture is established in history, leaving an imprint upon society. Some cultures will never change or embrace norms outside their historic systems. Exploring how cultures affect our churches, Dr. Chand identified five types of culture that I believe can be applied to any community: accepting, stoic, stagnant, embracing, or toxic.[2] Because you exist within a cultural community, the power of your culture contributes to your personal history, and possibly any inability to move beyond that history. Family, friends, ministry, and social norms all have input into our cultural makeup. Seeking cultural freedom is never easy if, to find it, you must break with history to escape a stagnant or toxic situation. One must break with cultural histories or risk living in a stagnant, controlling, toxic society.

My eldest brother loved life until his death, but he never believed in taking a risk. He believed life should be lived within confined areas. Without disrespect, I recall that he held one blue-collar job for nearly forty years prior to retirement. He purchased one new car in his entire life. He lived and died in the same house while new construction continued in his immediate area. My brother and I shared different views relative to history, and this created discomfort. He was uncomfortable with my aggressive professional moves. I failed the blue-collar test to become a meter reader at the company where he and my uncle worked. He thought having a job was sufficient, but I sought independence by owning my own firm. His fear kept him making safe choices to guarantee a paycheck. My ambition drove me to seek stock ownership and later become CEO of a company, leading a team of employees.

While I have the greatest respect for my hardworking brother, I can only imagine what he would have achieved had he let go of the cultural fear that kept him from taking risks in this life. He reacted to historic pain and fear, in this case fear of poverty or instability, and many of us do the same as we react to our culture. However, we can choose to react with hope rather than fear.

We must often overcome our cultural norms to claim a new life *after*. Africa and Israel vastly changed my cultural norms. I realized life is not simply a suburban home, two children, or an elite education. We change and diversify our culture by exploring other cultures; we seek them out and appreciate their values and accomplishments—even their fearlessness while living in poverty, enslavement, or bomb shelters. My earnest value for others' cultural history came to life while living in their shoes, if only for a moment.

Overcoming Childhood Mountains

Progress is never achieved until pain and sacrifice are present. Moving past historic painful memories is a process accomplished by deliberate dedication, commitment, and risk. The process is slow, methodical, and emotional. It's elastic, giving momentary releases followed by tighter constraints. Overcoming history is a lot like dieting. We often see few results initially, causing some to abandon a diet. Others know dieting requires patience, dedication, and consistency. Quick fixes or diet fads give false readings of success, but weight gain returns sevenfold. A conscious daily commitment to health is sure but slower than its fad counterpart. In the same way, walking thoughtfully through history produces permanent results or freedom.

I began this historic childhood transformation by accepting my father's death as tangible. Nearly thirty years after his departure, this mountain became real. Our minds possess an uncanny ability to suppress history until stimulated by an unexpected event. I was teaching several doctoral students and speaking on fulfilled dreams and ambitions. This discussion centered upon closing emotional gaps in our professional lives, instead of creating bridges to avoid them. This study stemmed from a Scripture on prosperity and being in good health: 3 John 1:2, "Beloved, I wish above all things that thou mayest prosper and be in health, even as thy soul prospereth." I was teaching that our lives are subject to voids, vacancies, and emptiness, and these gaps or voids exist where one loses the true meaning of prosperity. *After* sees prosperity as personal growth, happiness, and healthy living. Your value is not tied to your checking account balance.

One day, I was lecturing on the necessity of filling life gaps so as not to create vacancies within business or family; that's when history found me a second time. At that moment, thoughts of Andrew Carnegie Turner's absence flooded my mind. Never as a child or young adult had his absence so affected me. Some students in the class began sharing how their fathers shaped their lives, riding bikes together and playing baseball. This left me wondering what I had missed, and I felt called to visit my history seeking to understand his death and its impact on me. I spoke with my students about several things I'd missed, including not receiving a bicycle or red wagon from my dad. A few short weeks later, I found a red wagon neatly wrapped and sent to my office with a note reading, "Now you know how it feels to receive a red wagon." This poignant gesture reminded me that when it comes to our history, we can't un-ring a bell, but we can tell a new story based on that history. Dad's passing was historic, but I found his story living on as I passed it to my students, who engaged in new and caring ways. I never rode in the red wagon, but it closed a historic moment in my life.

History is an accurate accounting of your past. To find freedom, you must face that accurate account. Prayer and meditation provide space to think about historic moments of our lives. Journaling, reflection, and simply talking about the past can be fruitful as well. As we pray and meditate over the events of our past, our failures and tragedies, victories or losses may arise from this moment. Acknowledge this, but do not let it control your progress. In this way, history is a form of bondage creating fear against progress. What was your last disappointment? How trusting or mistrusting are you after your last shattering? Memory plays into our ability to move beyond our personal history. We must reclaim these memories—close the gaps—and resolve to live beyond them in positive ways.

Overcoming Domestic History

History often keeps us from restarting life or moving past previous mishaps. This is never truer than in our closest relationships—in our domestic histories. If statistics hold and nearly half of all marriages end in divorce, this issue will create a complex domestic history for many families. Divorce leaves us with strong memories long after the decree is signed. Divorce is a kind of domestic history that produces pain and hardships even after a marriage is dissolved. We are often ill-equipped to deal with the fallout; who enters marriage expecting its premature ending?

Divorce is commonplace, but few really understand the way this history affects our futures. The death of a marriage leaves a trail of shattered dreams, hopes, and desires. Domestic history affects the minds of others who witnessed the wedding ceremony but could not attend the court hearing. People once known as husband and wife are now plaintiff and defendant. Children are subject to shared custody, property is liquidated, assets are divided, savings are gone, and attorneys prosper as hearts bleed. Couples try desperately to place divorce firmly in their history, with marginal success. Matters of fault are argued in petitions and filings with local courts. Often civil communication is replaced with abusive dialogues, pain against pain, with no room for surrender or reconciliation. Regrets arrive quickly, leaving no room for forgiveness or healing.

While a decree gives legal freedoms to both plaintiff and defendant, they often struggle to move into the future. They move on, going separate directions, but are never completely removed from their past. Second marriages fail more often than first marriages because painful history makes spouses less likely to continue in the face of challenges. How can we find true, lasting freedom in the face of this painful, immediate history? How can this history be healed?

Of course, divorce is not the only piece of domestic history that affects individuals and families. Unhealthy home dynamics can be passed down from generation to generation. Conflict, tensions, and mistrust come from acts of betrayal and shortfalls from those closest to us. Yet painful history must not keep us from seeking peace and reconciliation. Moving on after a divorce, for example, starts with a simple prayer asking for peace—and it must include forgiveness. Peace leads to forgiveness and causes us to quit laying blame on the imperfect human beings who surround us. Life may be full of mishaps, disappointments, failures, and adverse memories. But starting again is possible. Finding a new partner is possible. Healing within a family is possible. Getting past the death of a father or mother is also possible. It all comes when we choose not to live in domestic history, but rather to move on in search of peace.

The Value of Peace

To find your *after* you must know the value of peace. Peace is our priceless commodity, but living in history restricts access to peace. We must fight for peace to clearly experience a new understanding and look into the future. Some dig in historic grave sites years after an event has happened, after a door is closed. They seek closure, but never leave the territory of history to build new things. Finding a new love or liberty is refreshing, bringing life to history. As I discovered on my trips to Africa and Israel, pain can produce passion and understanding, not bitterness.

In your cultural history, hold on to hope, open yourself to new cultures, and take a risk to change things. In your childhood history, find new ground and build from it to discover new strength. In your domestic history, seek peace, forgive, and look to the future. Patterns do not have to repeat themselves. And we can grow stronger and wiser once we face our history and move on. We can establish a new pattern—a pattern of peace. In this way, we can "forget those things which are behind," not out of avoidance or weakness, but out of a conscious choice to reach ahead into our future, straining on toward "the goal to win the prize for which God has called" us (Philippians 3:13–14).

Reflection Questions

1. What eras or stories from world history can you draw from to find strength? As if you are taking a trip to West Africa or Israel, find books or online resources to help you explore these historical moments and learn more about them.

_____

_____

_____

2. In what ways has your history inadvertently defined your future?

_____

_____

_____

3.   Take a moment to divide your personal history into "eras" or
     periods. What names would you give each of those eras? What
     characterizes each era?

     _____

     _____

     _____

4.   Now repeat the process for your cultural history, your childhood
     history, and your domestic history. What insights do you gain?

     _____

     _____

     _____

5.   What parts of your history do you need to "leave in the past"?

     _____

     _____

     _____

6.   What parts of your history can you use to fuel a better future?
     To inspire change and growth?

     _____

     _____

     _____

7.   What might it look like for you to find "peace" with your history?

     _____

     _____

     _____

CHAPTER 6

—— Clearing a Place to Build ——

In part one of this book, we discussed the many things we must "forget" or leave behind in order to "press onward," as we are encouraged in Philippians 3:13-14. Everything we've talked about is a form of what I like to call "waste removal," or removing debris in life in order to build again.

We can learn a great deal about waste removal from the story of Nehemiah.

Scripture tells us that Nehemiah was a leader who reacted in the face of a shattering moment for his people. The walls of their holy city, Jerusalem, had been destroyed and lay in ruins, and the remnant of Jews who lived there were without protection. Nehemiah was an Israelite who served as a cupbearer for a neighboring king. When he heard about the sad state of affairs, he "sat down and wept" (Nehemiah 1:4).

He pleaded with God to forgive his people and restore them. Nehemiah petitioned the king to let him return to Jerusalem and rebuild the wall. Armed with the king's blessing, he collected supplies, men, and guards for the journey, understanding his sole objective was to rebuild Jerusalem's destroyed walls. Nehemiah was not just an inspector; he became motivated to build, seeing the waste, hearing the opposition, all while depending upon the God of Israel.

Can you imagine the rubble he encountered when he arrived at the site? It must have seemed overwhelming, like a piece of crystal shattered beyond repair. Before he could rebuild, he had to deal with the debris.

In our lives, dealing with broken pieces is essential to moving forward. We must not allow shattered moments to leave unhealthy debris. Removing emotional debris is never easy—unlike physical rubbish, which is visible—but debris must be removed to expose damage and begin healing.

Nehemiah knew the enormity of his task and saw clearly that waste and debris had to be removed prior to rebuilding. The Bible tells us that to deal with this task, he approached the people for help. He said to the Israelites, "You see the trouble we are in: Jerusalem lies in ruins, and its gates have been burned with fire. Come, let us rebuild the wall of Jerusalem, and we will no longer be in disgrace" (1:17 NIV). They agreed, and to begin the enormous task they divided the wall into sections. Slowly, piece by piece, they began to rebuild. They began to see an *after* for the city of Jerusalem.

Perhaps you could see each chapter of this book so far as a section of wall for you to rebuild. We deal with the rubble of death in all its forms. We see debris from shattered moments. In our silence and solitude, we are tempted to sit down and rest on the rubble left by weariness, regret, loneliness, and isolation. And we face the rubble of history. The one thing we must do in our *after* is to clear a new place to build. *After* gives hope in the face of the shattered pieces of life. You are reading *After* because emotional debris is no longer welcome or has value. A bright future void of emotional waste or toxic behavior is in reach, and it has endless possibilities. Yesterday's debris is now powerless against this new future. Place this powerful truth into your vocabulary: "My future is greater than yesterday's sorrow."

Dividing the Wall

As a systems engineer, I learned that systematic order was critical to the success of every mission or goal in our aerospace firm. Many of our tasks were expansive, requiring complex logistics, strategic planning, coordination, and timely delivery of products and services. Slow delivery or slippage in one area was unacceptable, as it would adversely affect other areas. We knew unwanted delays were tied to a loss of profits for our corporation; a fiscal deficit would compromise our overall mission.

Life is a system, requiring attention to actions, behaviors, outside influences, relationships, and critical planning. Life without a plan is destined to become a life of mishaps or prolonged disappointments. Dreams and aspirations rise or die upon our ability to regain focus.

At this point in your life, consider yourself a Nehemiah, inspecting and dividing up a wall of rubble and making a plan to attack it piece by piece. You are finding new focus, but you will need a system and a relentless commitment to step-by-step progress. You can manage this project and see your walls rebuilt.

My late mother was a master of this kind of management. She was skilled at allotting time and not giving undue attention to unwanted waste. Mother Betty raised three families and was a strong proponent of progress. She did not linger in disappointments, neither did she rejoice in pain. Whenever one of her children suffered a setback, Mother Betty loved us back into the relationship with wisdom and we moved on.

As we begin to push away the rubble of life, we must begin to see the future over the mounds of debris. We must be like Mother Betty and not linger in disappointments, preferring instead to build life. Great cities could be built on the ground you are clearing. Your approach must be systematic; you must make planned moves and work strategically to finish the impossible.

"I Cannot Go Down"

As Nehemiah began systematically managing his massive project, he faced opposition. Enemies tried to sabotage and distract him. They tried to get him to come down off the wall and parlay with them. Instead, Nehemiah said, "They were scheming to harm me; so I sent messengers to them with this reply: 'I am carrying on a great project and cannot go down. Why should the work stop while I leave it and go down to you?' Four times they sent me the same message, and each time I gave them the same answer" (Nehemiah 6:3 NIV).

He would not even speak with them. He wouldn't stop his important work. As you remove the rubble to rebuild your life, enemies will rise up to distract you as well—and more than four times. To each one of them you must say, "I am doing a great work, and I cannot go down." Remain focused, and you will prevail despite the voices of these common enemies.

The Enemies of Mistrust and Bitterness

Mistrust, as we have discussed, is a crippling enemy, and listening to its voice can lead to a greater debilitation called bitterness. Mistrust is often devalued because it can become an excuse for leaving waste in our lives. Thoughts of mistrust normally overshadow our ability or willingness to make decisions. Some pridefully say they will never trust another man or woman after a divorce or relationship mishap. This statement ends hope, giving way to bitterness.

We can never reach success while distracted or crippled by bitterness. Bitterness is a place designed to keep you from experiencing *after*. When bitterness and mistrust rage, remember your work and say, "I will not stop this great work to reason with you."

The Enemy of Unfairness

"Life is not fair." I'm sure you've heard this statement many times in your life, and it never gets less true. The voice of unfairness will call to you, reminding you of all you have lost. It will try to get you to stop the great work of rebuilding your life, removing the rubble, and moving on. And it is often tempting to go down to it. It is tempting to reminisce and grieve, to stop the work, but we must not. Grief has its place—even Nehemiah wept when he heard about Jerusalem and its people. But he did not stay in quarantine or stop his great work in order to dwell in the tragedy of it all.

As I surveyed the rubble in my life, I was almost overwhelmed with the unfairness of it. Mother's death came with pain, but we expected it. My wife and I were married nineteen months from beginning to end before she died of advanced liver cancer. Both women passed within months of each other.

I learned of my wife's cancer two weeks before our elaborately planned wedding was to take place. Our secret pain was masked beneath pageantry, guests, and gala activities. Nothing prepared me for the upcoming storm. I went from tuxedo to oncology within forty-eight hours. Nineteen months later I was standing at her grave site giving a final kiss to her casket.

When I reached out to two of my closet friends, they were unequipped to support me, leaving me relegated to my own silence and grief. *Life is not fair* became my refrain. And it did not let up.

With much pain I learned that picking up your life requires a decision. Follow your heart when silence prevails. The wisdom that follows will outweigh others' opinions or your immediate understanding. The voices of unfairness can lead to anger or to the desire to give up. If this is your situation, know that yes, it is unfair in our eyes, but just to the Master. When unfairness calls to you on the wall, you might very well agree with what it has to say. But you must tell unfairness, "I am doing a good work and cannot come down!"

The Enemy of Impatience

I must repeat: rebuilding your life's dreams is a tedious process. It's a series of deliberate steps, approaches, and efforts set in motion to reach your desired end point. Our greatest opposition in this era is not the process but rather finding the patience required to reach an end point. We are often defeated by our own inconsistency and inability to measure our fights and conquer our impatience. David measured his battles or fights by evaluating his enemies' spoils or treasure. Never go into battle when your enemy lacks spoils. Measure the wealth of your battle; if it is purely emotional without compensation, leave quickly. If it reunites you with family, children, or some other valued resource, fight for it.

As you stand upon your wall, as you clear the rubble, know the voices that call to you in opposition. Perhaps you are most likely to:

- overreact and rely on unstable emotions;

- lack patience, wanting results without having facts;

- seek support for your position rather than seeking guidance for truth;

- evaluate last and react first;

- forget that rebuilding or repositioning is a systematic process; or

- choose easily accessible solutions or partners for comfort.

But now that you recognize those voices, you can deny them as soon as they reach your ears.

In the next section, we continue to build and overcome. We will go from "forgetting what is behind" to "straining toward what is ahead," from clearing the rubble to laying the bricks of a new life. And as you walk into your *after* systematically, bravely, and one step at a time, you will begin to see a new structure taking place.

We all wish to experience life without shattering events. When life begins to take you where you don't want to go, remember each place can bring you value and experience. Avoid bitterness and regret.

Learn how to express desire for life instead of calculating the waste that lies before you. Plan your wall instead of dwelling on the rubble. And always remember, you are built to last in a place called *after*.

Reflection Questions

1. In part one of this book, what have you learned about the "waste" that needs to be removed in your life?

_____

_____

_____

_____

2. What do the actions of Nehemiah teach us about how to approach waste removal?

_____

_____

_____

_____

3. In "rebuilding the wall" of your life, what "sections" can you identify?

_____

_____

_____

_____

4.   Take these sections and write them down. What rubble or debris will you need to clear out before rebuilding each of these sections?

_____

_____

_____

5.   What voices or enemies are you most prone to listening to while you are at work rebuilding?

_____

_____

_____

6.   What strategic plan can you make to deny distractions from mistrust, bitterness, unfairness, and impatience in each of your "sections"?

_____

_____

_____

7.   Encourage yourself in the Lord. Seek out and write down a Scripture of encouragement for each of your "sections," as well as words to remember when inevitable "enemies" try to impede your progress. How do the tools discussed in part one equip you in each of these sections?

_____

_____

_____

PART 2

Straining Toward What Is Ahead

*Brothers and sisters, I do not consider myself yet to have taken hold of it. But one thing I do: Forgetting what is behind and **straining toward what is ahead**, I press on toward the goal to win the prize for which God has called me heavenward in Christ Jesus.*

Philippians 3:13–14 NIV

CHAPTER 7

Changed

Change is unavoidable and constant, much like sunrise or sunset—both never cease to exist. Change is part of our life. Whether it's a sudden drastic change, or the steady long-term change of seasons, embracing it remains problematic for some, who resist change. We will face two kinds of change in life: unwanted and conscious change. One happens *to* you, the other happens by design.

You may be experiencing the fallout of adverse, unwanted change. Perhaps it has happened suddenly, in a manner beyond your control; or slowly, creeping up on you almost unnoticed. Unwanted changes can leave you asking, "Who have I become? Who am I after this change that I didn't ask for?" In your *after*, you can counter unwanted change by responding with calculated, conscious changes—planned modifications designed to make you better, not bitter. In Paul's letter to the Romans he encouraged followers to avoid conforming to this world but be transformed by the renewing of the mind (Romans 12:1–2). The renewal of your mind is a conscious change. Conscious change is evolutionary; it occurs in stages until *after* is the new normal. Priceless experiences are acquired through conscious change. Collect positive memories while in this season of life.

Slow Change

If you have watched a caterpillar transform into a butterfly, you have witnessed slow change. His transformation happens through a series of precise, though gradual, natural processes. In his time in the cocoon, he has limited vision, and he hangs vulnerable to his natural enemies. But when he emerges, he is a thing of beauty—a creature capable of full flight. His slow, systematic changes have produced positive outcomes.

Conversely, many of us have witnessed slow change for the worse. It may start with a traumatic moment, but a negative "natural" process begins, creating a slow build-up of anxiety, depression, or thoughts of death. If it is not stopped or addressed, it can have tragic consequences.

In recent years, suicidal incidents have become commonplace as more and more prominent individuals confront the negative evolution of lingering pain. The caterpillar possesses an internal stimulus that guides him through this rigorous transformative process. Humans, on the other hand, often become wearied by unsuspecting or unscheduled changes, whether the death of family or friends, or failed businesses or marriages. Without a guide or stimulus, humans will struggle with transformative change.

I recently learned of a prominent thirty-year-old pastor here in Southern California who became one of the many professionals, pastors, and laity who vigorously toil with unscheduled changes in their lives. My heart ached while reading his wife's account of his bouts with depression and anxiety, which led him to attempt suicide while in the church office. His first attempt led to final conclusion in his home. He left behind three young sons, a wife, and a large congregation. Unresolved issues can cause unspeakable grief. *After* seeks to address these issues before they become dangerous.

Paul speaks of this private warfare: "I see another law in my members, warring against the law of my mind, and bringing me into captivity to the law of sin which is in my members" (Romans 7:23).

In this chapter we will discuss how to strengthen the "law of the mind" over the "law of the members." Renewing a mind is critical when in turmoil; change, if not managed, will manipulate its foe until captivity or premature death occurs. When we respond to unwanted change with an *after* mind-set, we can come through transformed, like the butterfly. The *after* mind-set is transformative: it provides clear directions with deliberate responses to unplanned life changes. Caterpillars possess transformative mind-sets; butterflies take flight.

In an Instant

Life changed instantly; this cliché is vividly etched into my being. October 1, 2017, brought unplanned change with severity. That day a friend mourned the death of his adoring ninety-plus-year-old mother. That loss was underscored with a mass shooting in Las Vegas, Nevada. In minutes, fifty-nine individuals succumbed to gunfire, leaving them mortally wounded, while another six hundred were wounded. The massive moments that killed and destroyed families and friends left tragic scars in an instant. Our mothers were not cut down instantly, but death without warning is severe.

My friend's mother quietly transitioned from this life into heavenly hands as her loving family stood bedside.

That day, death's trajectory forged an unplanned transitional memory for many who stood on concert grounds without knowing an instant event would forever change their lives.

Death remains painful, whether slow or swift. It continues to mark those who remain. Tears from a son or tears from a husband—these all fall fresh when death announces its entry.

Who are you now, post-October 1, 2017? We have varied dates, but the question remains valid. Are there visible, tangible changes, or are they hidden underneath deep scars? A series of unplanned events may cause involuntary changes of character, demeanor, and temperament. Going forward is necessary; why not bcome stronger and grow from this moment onward? Yes, it is painful—perhaps feels impossible—to recover. *After* is power to recover and rebuild.

Rebuilding the Pyramid

In 1943, psychologist Abraham Maslow introduced his "hierarchy of needs." This theory underscores a sequential order of intrinsic needs that must be met before reaching self-actualization. Maslow's bottom-up theory is presented in the form of an inverted triangle or pyramid, with the most basic needs at the base, and then subsequent needs built on top. At the base, you have physical needs (food, water, air, health). Once those are met, you can address security needs (safety, shelter, stability). After that comes social needs (love, belonging, inclusion), then self-esteem needs (ego, power, recognition), and then finally, at the top of the pyramid, self-actualization. Self-actualization occurs when all independent levels are stabilized, and a fulfilled life is accomplished.[3]

Maslow's theory considers static order, but change affects his theory; impacts occur, causing undesirable outcomes. Removing or changing basic shelter, water, utilities, or food at the base of the pyramid results in sorrow and pain. (Think of the terrible devastation that comes with a hurricane, when the basics of life are blown away.) It becomes impossible to reach self-actualization or become productive without basic elements of life.

Maslow's theory is vulnerable to instant unforeseen impacts, such as those of October 1, 2017; a child born with cancer cells; a family member's sudden transition; or an uptick in suicides. These impacts will alter Maslow's theory instantly. Basic needs exist, but sipping water, bathing, and eating all become less desirable; this rebuilding process is necessary, though not easy.

This stimulates fact and bypasses fiction. Are leaders born or trained? Are you innately capable of recovering from instant, unforeseen impacts or is *after* the training ground? My peers supported me in matrimony, knowing that stage four cancer was making its way. They supported me with presence but not one had verbal instruction. They attended our elaborate wedding and then nineteen months later returned for her solemn funeral. I now have *after*, an experience and voice to support others who have faced a sudden death.

Use *after* to acquire inspiration while observing those in Las Vegas or Puerto Rico. They championed this: "We shall rebuild and continue. Circumstances will not weaken our authentic beings." Enduring change creates a stronger, resilient, authentic being as it produces value to help others based upon your new view of life. Material elements give way to healing, recovery, and inspirational hope.

After produces an authentic being, one who realizes change is constant and impacts will occur and yet remains confident in God, knowing everything is subject to unforeseen moments of life.

The Authentic You

We are moving now from theory to practice. Theory is easy; someone on the outside of your painful change can give you any amount of advice, but it is always easier said than done. Now, to survive, you are grappling with the realities of life, realities of change, and realities of your needs, and facing those realities stabilizes your authentic being. The heavy lifting will leave you stronger.

Now theory becomes knowledge and experience. These life experiences, no matter where they came from, will authentically change our lives. We will become more authentic people in response.

Divorce and cancer taught me about the realities of change and the authenticity that comes from it. Neither event came with an instruction manual or schedule. Divorce feels like doing heart surgery with a spoon. It never ends and it's extremely dulling. You become anesthetized after a while; emotions vary from sheer shock to anger, fear, fighting, and even foolishness. We never plan for a death to marriage. Ex-spouses become jaded, untrusting, cynical, and withdrawn, and they experience emotional trauma. Reaching self-actualization becomes problematic, because catastrophic change has occurred further down the pyramid, and we don't have the skill sets we need to rebuild. Some never recover. But you must rebuild, starting with forgiveness and move into authenticating your new self-worth.

Choosing to leave sorrow, pain, and life's "messy" choices is often difficult as one fights against internal moral theologies. We tend to move slowly or with caution, often wondering if freedom does exist. Can true love or peace exist following seasons of battle or turmoil? This is when we must change must become purposeful. Self-worth requires deliberate movement with intentionality, knowing healing is a time-released process. We begin to heal as we go, and we experience a new level of confidence moving forward.

Losing a loved one to cancer changed the footprint of my life. My experience with cancer was cruel, dark, and painful. I was not the patient, but my wife's pain changed me. No one is adequately prepared for this devastating disease. While the medications robbed her of life, depleted red blood cells, and turned soft skin into coarse leather, her body changed. Our outlook on life changed as well. But in those final days, we treasured the small, real moments that last in our memories. It revealed what was authentic.

As you walk through your changing moments, look for realities while in meditation; these reveal treasures of life or authentic values. Life displays real treasures after a loss. Let them show you what is real, and you will have gained something valuable.

What Keeps Us from Changing?

History remains history; past must lead to our future. Historic or present elements of life produce biological and emotional change. Lemons become great in Arnold Palmers and lemon pie, and they enhance seafood with a simple slice. Better is coming!

Life changes will ring a bell that you can't un-ring. What has happened, has happened. After moments like these we are changed, and we must change ourselves in response. Still, many people put two fingers in one ear and pretend not to have heard that life-changing ring. Let's acknowledge its presence and move forward. Being emotionally upset is normal as grief works its process in our lives. But refusing to acknowledge or adapt to change is counterproductive. It provides room for addictions and depression. Don't make this mistake.

Bitterness

Bitter or Better: these two come alongside changes of life, offering their wares. The latter is complex; it requires work and dedication along with support systems. Bitterness is autonomous, offers no value, needs little external support or justification. Bitterness destroys past and future relationships, constrains creativity, alters communication, affects cognitive thinking, and infects everything within your space. Bitter individuals have chained their hearts to adverse circumstances or their past. They vilify themselves, live in captivity, avoid inspirational-healing moments with volumes of mistrust. Bitterness is an abstract, negative power dwelling within our hearts, but it is contagious. It justifies cruelty. It changes our hearts, slowly, for the worse. Bitterness begets more bitterness and can only be stopped with prayer and forgiveness. Prayer and forgiveness will unwrap bitterness. Watch out for a root of bitterness in your life, and act to stop it before it begins to grow. Pray as David did, "Create in me a pure heart, O God, and renew a steadfast spirit within me" (Psalm 51:10 KJV). Turn to God and ask Him to defend you from bitterness.

Bitterness comes naturally, but "better" is a choice. It is an action. It's a conscious change. We must make a concerted effort to become better. We must decide not to linger in tragic events. Death, divorce, destruction—all must be met with a definitive declaration: "I will not lose determination." When change comes, accept its invitation. Move with change; embrace change; follow and flow with change. And let it make you better, not bitter.

Fear of Others

Change can produce fear. Our facade portrays stability, but underneath, fear is working, weakening positions of faith, favor, and bright futures. This leads us into isolation. Let's live full of courage, determined to conquer fear.

An authentically free being is known by their air of hope, assurance, encouragement for others—knowing that depression, sickness, death, or failure were elements in their lives. They are overcomers!

The other people in our lives can help us discover this. Take inventory of those in your inner circle. Evaluate the culture you are permitting in your life, and take stock of who is toxic and who is inspirational. You will have to fight a fierce battle to choose better over bitter, and you will need help on your side.

External support is critical to avoiding bitterness. Find someone who has become authentically free. You can tell who is authentically free because they will have an air of hope, though they may face depression, sickness, death, or failure. Authentic freedom is seldom discovered until it has become a witness to others. Facebook or other social media platforms do not advertise who is "authentically free." During my paralysis and resulting surgery, two individuals proved themselves to be true, free friends. They never left my side, providing words of encouragement and life from authentic points of view. It is no coincidence that each of them had experienced loneliness, loss, rejection, or some form of severe change. Their voices and words of "authentic freedom" created whispers of life while facing death.

Speak to someone who has undergone shatterings but is whole again. Do not allow insecurities to prohibit new relationships, even if those relationships are temporary. Some relationships are seasonal, like scaffolds on a building. They are there for a moment, not for a lifetime, to help you rebuild.

Transformative thinking is critical to moving forward. Become a forward thinker by restructuring the culture in which you live and work, and specifically those who make up your inner circle. Look at the mind-sets and activities of those in your inner circle. Are they forward thinkers? Do they constantly display apathy or lethargic life patterns? The key here is not to change them, but to change circles. Perhaps changing circles is not possible for you now. If you cannot change the circle, change your personal perspective by defining your core values. (We will talk more about this in the next chapter.)

Some people spend years seeking acceptance from peers or other professional circles. This desire is admirable if the community is whole and healthy. Too often our discomfort or prolonged pain comes from emotional longing for acceptance and love. But as you seek out new relationships, remember that love, friendships, and relationships are reciprocal. Don't bother trying to please those who are consumed by bitterness.

Remember, "God so loved the world that He *gave* ..." (John 3:16). He did not just take but He gave, showing us authentic unbiased love. Giving of yourself becomes enjoyable when the recipient loves and respects your authenticity. Do not give to get, but you will receive because you are giving in the correct environment. Let others help, not hinder you as you walk forward into change.

Disappointments

Another trap in life occurs when we give excessive attention to a single disappointment. One rejection, act of disrespect, discomfort, or disgraceful attempt must not end your quest for a better life. Regrets are acceptable, but holding yourself responsible for extended periods can be damaging. One of my students shared with me the story of her regrets. As she shared, it became evident that her experience turned into self-inflicted pain, and the cycle was continuing. Her regrets were multiplying. Self-inflicted pain has a long-lasting effect that can be even greater than external pain, so we must be vigilant about holding on to disappointments. Every single individual on this planet has made bad decisions. But we must move on. Despite my own personal regrets and disappointments I have resolved to live every day enjoying the love of family, the hope of a dedicated partner, and finding new business partnerships with people of integrity.

Our future is directly connected to the determination in our hearts, minds, and spirits. To find your *after*, embrace today. Let's determine not to allow our bright futures to be tainted by past mistakes. Giving up your future due to the opinions of others or lingering memories of your past is futile. Winning requires overpowering the opinions of others. Today is a new day full of new expectations. Doors of opportunity swing open daily. Why not believe they are opening toward you and your future?

Tools for Change

Now that you know what to avoid, collect tools to help you walk through your change. When you feel hesitant, afraid, or on the verge of becoming bitter, commit to taking action and making the conscious change for "better" instead. Remember, this doesn't happen on its own. It takes your active participation to change for the better.

Encourage Yourself

Self-encouragement is one of life's greatest priceless assets; its investment pays high dividends.

But if it hasn't occurred, do not wait on external encouragement; it may or may not come. Invest in yourself when others fail to invest. Cheers for you may become silent while embracing *after*; buy a whistle and blow it. Applaud yourself, who truly understands progress, until they rest in your pain or discomfort.

In 1 Samuel 30:8, David asked the Lord if he should pursue his enemy who had taken his wives, his wealth, and all that was deemed valuable. "David inquired of the Lord, 'Shall I pursue this raiding party? Will I overtake them?' 'Pursue them,' he answered. 'You will certainly overtake them and succeed in the rescue.' "

David exhibited the principle of finding courage while others sought to kill and destroy. Purposeful living knows the value of moving forward while facing conflict. Pursuit is a form of encouraging oneself, or asking for that next level of vital strength to acquire all that is yours. This level of determination may or may not come from your peers. Be grateful when it does, be determined if it does not. Encourage yourself in the Lord.

We have authority in our tongue, power to speak life when in sickness, light when in darkness, or peace while in storms. The pure prayer will reach the heart of God.

The Power of Confidence

Confidence isn't in-born. The good news is, you can build it. Having confidence is often criticized as arrogance or being self-centered. But real confidence actually comes from long journeys through disappointments, heartbreaks, setbacks, or even some addictive behaviors. It's a moment in time when you awaken and realize something inside you is made of stronger stuff.

Confidence is built through failed attempts and repeatedly deciding to keep going. My sister, Ida Mae, was a confidence builder because she continuously spoke affirming words into my life. Ida Mae was a professional homemaker and mother of nine, and she knew how to be inspirational. I followed Ida Mae's advice and moved with confidence to Washington, DC, and the rest is history. Confidence led me away from a blue-collar town with dead-end opportunities into the nation's capital with endless opportunities. Confidence led me into pre-law, then into politics, and eventually into leading an aerospace firm to launch E & I Systems as the president and founder. Perhaps you have a wonderful career, yet you are feeling less than fulfilled. Pursue confidence, and become acquainted with risk. Take the leap and establish your passion, and the rest will become history.

Making the first move toward confidence is difficult. But whenever you sense a strong internal pull into uncharted waters, that's a clue that your confidence is near. So why not risk it all and become the best in your *after*?

Building confidence in the absence of a mentor is possible. Confidence is simply being secure. It does not require perfection or speed; it merely starts with internal honesty. Face your fears and laugh at failures. Failure is a day in time; use it to gain principles, and think of it as a child's first steps. Confidence deals with pain while accepting its tears of sorrow. Do not live with denial; admit that losing a job, contract, ministry, or loved one is painful. Confidence declares if breath remains, so does confidence or ability to return with wisdom and courage. Speak life to yourself. As Ida Mae laid the foundation in me, you too can build upon those values.

Patience and confidence go hand in hand. Success rarely comes quickly, but rather with the determination of an ant. Have you ever seen an ant who is determined not to lose a bit of cake even when the cake is larger than its body mass? Ants are patient when pulling spoils into their nests. And they certainly don't lack confidence, comparing themselves to the size of that crumb! Perhaps we can learn from them not to be overtaken by our challenges due to their size. With confidence and patience, we can embrace change.

Be Fueled

Commercial airliners are amazing wonders. To fly, they depend on fuel tanks that are strategically housed in the wings of the aircraft. Each tank is a contributor to the whole fuel system. If fuel from one tank becomes compromised, it does not compromise the entire flight. We are able to continue flying using fuel from another source without having to land prematurely. In the same way, if you are properly fueled, failures or changes in one section of your life do not require a total shutdown, just a switch to another source to continue your journey.

You have four distinct tanks to draw from:

1. the past

2. the present

3. your future, and

4. endless opportunities.

To find our *after*, we often have to shut down our history tank, pull from our present, and hope for the future. Staying in the present is possible, but you must not allow your toxic past to pipe unwanted fuel into your system. Toxic behavior should be addressed immediately so your fuel is not tainted. Toxic behaviors are repetitive decisions or choices you make, knowing the outcome will be negative. One young adult described to me her toxic behavior of being in constant conversation with someone who has declared his disdain for her. He continues to call, and she continues to receive the calls with new levels of frustration.

Most past toxic behaviors are habits that provide little benefit compared to extreme levels of personal waste or heartache. Shut down that tank. Identify those behaviors, and draw good fuel for a better life.

Those who are fueled by vibrant lives with positive outlooks are not eager to draw from a faulty tank. As you face change, continue to draw on the tank of hope, and you will find yourself soaring into your *after*.

Everything Must Change

Songwriter James Ingram wrote a classic anthem titled "Everything Must Change." He speaks poetically with these lyrics:

> Everything must change
> Nothing stays the same
> Everyone will change
> No one stays the same

Since change is certain, be ready for it. And have confidence, knowing that each unwanted change can trigger a new and powerful voluntary change in your life. Perhaps you'll learn a new skill in response to your change. Perhaps you'll become an expert in something you never would have considered before. Or you'll discover authenticity amid pain. Or find a new community of supporters and advisors when you realize you must reach out for help. You will adapt, streamline, and become better, not bitter. I hope that you will become a master of change, not a victim of change, and grow flexible, discerning, and confident. After all, if you are to find your *after,* you must decide it's time for a change.

———— ✦ ————

Reflection Questions

1. Can you identify a slow change for the better in your life? A slow change for the worse?

   _____

   _____

   _____

2. What involuntary changes are you grappling with right now?

   _____

   _____

   _____

3. How can a voluntary change help you transform through those negative events?

   _____

   _____

   _____

4. When have you experienced a change on Maslow's pyramid? How did that affect you?

   _____

   _____

   _____

5. How has unwanted change in your life made you resilient or
    authentic?

    _____

    _____

    _____

6. In what ways do you find yourself resistant to change?

    _____

    _____

    _____

7. What tools for change will you employ to help you become better
    instead of bitter in your time of change? How will you employ
    them?

    _____

    _____

    _____

CHAPTER 8

Staging Your Brand Comeback

B *rands.* You see them everywhere. Our economy is based upon societies' acceptance or rejection of a brand. Brands send powerful messages using symbols in lieu of words, and global response to these symbols is massive. A red and white box with KFC printed on it is extremely powerful even in Trinidad; the Golden Arches are powerful in Europe; global branding is expanding. No matter where we are, we interact with brands every day of our lives. We are loyal to them because they symbolize something to us, whether it's trustworthiness, quality, taste, or style. When familiar brands make changes in their branding, we often react strongly. When a brand or business takes a downturn, it often undergoes "rebranding," or refurbishment of looks, logos, messages, advertising, and ethos. Increasingly we hear about sports stars and entertainers "branding" and rebranding themselves, or marketing themselves as a business based on their personal values. But branding is not just for companies and celebrities. You can learn much from the business world as you find your *after.* Brands make comebacks, so why not you?

Roy T. Bennett said, "Other people's perception of you is a reflection of them; your response to them is an awareness of you."[4] In the same vein, another popular quote tells us, "When you can't control what's happening, challenge yourself to control the way you respond to what's happening. That's where your power is."[5] Rebranding is a way of responding to what has happened to you. In your *after,* you will begin to respond to your situation in a way that looks to the future. Make strategic decisions about your brand—how you want to be recognized—and you can orchestrate your comeback. Why not change or become a brand rather than a victim of circumstances?

Branding centers upon a message. It conveys powerful imagery for those who observe a person, place, or thing. Branding has become a new staple in defining your *after* instead of just your name. The latter is a legal representation of your personhood, while a brand sets you apart from others with a strong conviction, message, and revitalized character.

Several years ago Hostess Cupcake fell prey to economic downsizing. The *Wall Street Journal* began running stories about its impending demise. The Hostess brand was an institution in many American homes. As a result, consumers who followed the company could not accept the demise of the beloved Twinkie. After many business maneuvers, the Hostess Twinkie returned complete with a label on each package that said, "The sweetest comeback ever."

Do we believe life is less valuable than cupcakes? Twinkies made a triumphant return; now it's your turn to make a "sweet comeback."

You have a unique opportunity to associate a comeback with your brand. Far too many give way to disappointment, failed marriages, financial despair, sickness, lawsuits, or a host of setbacks and problems. If we accept death in these areas, we stop ourselves from coming back. Hostess decided to avoid defeat, so it turned its consumers' disappointment into a victory.

After is your personal "sweetest comeback ever." There's no better time than now to begin your journey into the endless opportunities awaiting a creative mind. A brand depicts your story, not your circumstances. You are not looking for handouts, but your hand will be held high with victory.

Brand Recognition

Branding is greater than just a catchy phrase or ad campaign to manipulate buyers to purchase a product. Renewed perspective creates a brand, not just a name. A brand is symbolic of strength or durability; it gives recognition beyond your name. What do you want people to associate with your brand?

Mars Candy is a company, but M&M is its flagship brand. These little pieces of chocolate are craved and beloved around the world, and we all recognize what their branding stands for. Branding establishes its presence in today's marketplace, but also defines the capacity to compete. Other chocolates exist, but the M&M brand has established presence in tomorrow's market share; few other brands have the recognizability and durability Mars has worked so hard to establish.

My University of Southern California mentor, Reverend Dr. Cecil Murray, defined branding as having three elements: purpose, provisions, and resources to accomplish each.

Purpose is one's lifelong duty or your God-ordained direction. Purposeful individuals view time, desires, or disappointments through the lens of a greater goal. A key element to purpose is understanding the difference between disappointment and determination. No one is immune to disappointments; even Christ processed His on numerous occasions. Yet His purpose or God-ordained direction provided fuel to continue. Life offers endless crossroads with alternatives called individuality or free choice. Purpose stimulates one's inner core while facing opposition or challenge.

Resources and provisions are alike yet distinguishable. Provisions come from our determination to believe impossibilities, much like miracles. Resources are the immediate content of one's possessions, which is often less than the need. Our dreams and passions are financed through the perceptions of our purpose instead of a meager balance in one's account or one's credit score. Our Father honors His Word and works best when purpose-driven individuals find their *after.*

Dr. Murray's lectures on this topic raised our awareness that we were not just individuals, but could become an establishment or brand. Dr. Murray spoke from authority, because he was a powerful brand himself. He pioneered the Los Angeles renaissance period following massive rioting and community unrest. His accomplishments created a brand on USC campus; the Cecil Murray Center for Community Engagement has an established name, but his brand speaks of one who has stood in the fire. He is revered for his tenacity, having come from rural beginnings to lead hundreds of thousands of students. He created a brand of strength from suffering. While others were reaching for handouts, he began philanthropic efforts to give others a hand, to provide insight to those less fortunate individuals. His brand recognition at USC is powerful and enduring.

Dr. Murray shows us that greatness is never achieved without sacrifice; it often follows adversity and can produce a very powerful brand. Let us explore more of what branding could mean for you, as you define your purpose and identify potential resources for your brand comeback.

Purpose

What is the purpose of your brand? What is your mission statement in life? What are your core values? At the beginning of every brand is a purpose. Dr. Cecil Murray's purpose for the Center for Community Engagement, for example, is "to equip faith leaders to transform underserved communities."[6] It's simple, straightforward, and powerful. It states a need, an action, and a solution. As you contemplate your *after,* consider what your purpose might be.

Ask yourself: What are the foundational reasons you want to reset or rebrand your life? What is your greater value/calling? How are you called to serve, in light of what has happened to you? Your greatest purpose is strategically assigned to your greatest pain.

Purpose can be found in service. Servanthood distinguishes victims from helpers. Most effective servants have once been victims in some way, so they bring passion and perspective along with a helping hand. Serving is giving back to others with a cause, not with a motive or agenda. Servanthood asks, "How may I be of service by giving of myself to others in need of hope or new direction?" These individuals offer help, care, or compassion, knowing their service emanates from real experience instead of ideals and theories.

First responders are servants; they sacrifice to give to others in need. They bring heartfelt compassion to the battlefields of life not for self-glory but to give glory through giving. Through this giving, they become part of something bigger than an individual. They become part of a purpose—a mission. Your brand is a reflection of that mission.

How can you be a "first responder" in your situation? What will your responses—your actions—tell others about your brand or purpose? The motivation behind your responses will help build the kind of brand recognition you can be proud of. Be dedicated to responding effectively with new ideas and positive motivation. When others hear your name, you want them to know your purpose and to connect it with attributes of character, wisdom, vitality, and endurance that will make up your *after*.

Resources

Rebranding takes resources. And in the world of business, that means money and people: money in the form of investors and capital, and people having leadership qualities, integrity, and professional cadence. In your personal rebranding, you will need to assess your resources. It will mean thinking about your relationship to money and physical resources. It will mean evaluating your nonmonetary, internal resources such as personal strength and determination. And it will mean evaluating the people in your life. When all these elements work together, your resources turn into strength and power. Learn to seek out and attract the right resources, and your brand can symbolize not only your purpose, but the power to back it up.

Money

It's undeniable: money matters. Money is a silent giant that interrupts so many people trying to regain hope or inspiration in life. I feel compelled to address this topic because it is critical to understand: *resetting life is not tied to fiscal capacity*. Writing on this topic is personal for me; my perspective comes from years of reaching beyond immediate dollar resources to accomplish unpredictable goals and objectives. A personal belief system or brand outweighs bank account balances or assets. Branding begins to take shape with determination as a believer and dreamer. Persistence eventually produces provision.

Life must not be controlled solely by your current access to money, but your branding ability may give you access to wealth. Lacking money is not an excuse not to reset your life. Most startup business owners obtain contributions from family and friends, knowing traditional banks will not underwrite dreams. I began my business with family loans and a trunk for office space. More than money, creativity is your currency. Using creativity, you can begin to look for resources in unexpected places. Creativity is priceless, and it is freedom for those who are searching for *after*.

If you are experiencing money-related woes, I encourage you to see yourself as wealthy while waiting for an influx of money. I formulated my first business, E & I Systems Engineering Firm, with no capital, a twenty-five (25) percent interest-rate loan from my parents, and another five-hundred-dollar loan from friends. E & I Systems later became a Small Business Administration 8A certified for-profit corporation with offices throughout the northeast region of the United States. This task was not easy. It would have been much easier if I'd had massive startup capital or money from a family trust. Our circumstances are often limited to concepts, dreams, and passions without capital. But there's a point where determination must override economic lack. To get there, we must first overcome a poverty mind-set.

Our American society suggests we are all created equal, but equality is relative to one's ability to escape the poverty of our mind-set. Poverty is not only a measurement of financial wealth or the lack thereof, but it is also a factor of our branding—the personal message we associate with ourselves. Rising from the ashes of poverty is never easy, but it does happen. You must pursue or become hungry for "better" until better is presented. This is a personal goal, and it's never obtained without a push.

After is a push through your pain, abuses, and years of disrespect or rejection. Your comeback establishes determination, and power is derived from life's negatives. Many have endured the loss of financial security or being manipulated by schemes or unforeseen turns in their professional arena. Let's brand a new life objective, walk into it, and become powerfully focused. Secure your brand and make changes where needed; perhaps just learn to say no without feeling guilty.

A creative mind and your internal drive are signs of a dreamer who is creating a brand. Waiting for external support is self-defeating and oppressive; no one is going to approach you with a bank account full of capital or ideas to jumpstart your personal brand comeback. But as you determine your brand, you begin to define what symbolizes the sum total of who you are (your purpose) and what you bring to the marketplace (the need you serve). Then you can begin to push and create a consumer's desire to partner with you in the marketplace—to connect your skills with other people's need. This can often bring with it opportunities and, yes, monetary resources. Branding creates a desire for your product or services, which in turn brings sustainability and strength.

People

A powerful, accomplished organization contains people and money. These resources are interwoven; both are essential to success. The people around you make up your culture, and a rich culture is inspirational. A company's brand typically follows the culture of its environment. So if your culture or those around you embrace negative experiences with dark stories, no doubt your brand will symbolize darkness and defeat. Brands can be inspirational, or they can be doomed. Defining your brand will require a look at your stakeholders—those who contribute to your thought process and provide inspiration. If they are toxic, so will be their contributions.

This is never truer than when you are rising up from oppression, trouble, defeat, or a shattering event. Defeat is an attitude without a battle. And culture shapes that attitude and controls our responses to others. The oppressed individual's culture influences his or her "bounce-back resolve"; it affects motivational levels. Inspirational cultures encourage us and provide strength to face opposing moments.

An inspirational, healthy culture is needed to produce a strong successful brand. Do one thing different: become engaged with assets or positive minds outside your immediate area. Open up your life to people from all walks of life. Be determined to seek out people who have like spirits, personalities, ambition, and drive. Expand your focus audience; go beyond people who share your heritage, race, socioeconomic background, or geographical affiliations. You want to have people in your life who believe in endless possibilities. These individuals will give sound advice without fear; they will support your strengths and identify your weaknesses simultaneously. Invite creative people into your world and find those who bring solutions with problems; these are vital contributors. The world is full of people who can identify a problem; brand power says we see the problem and create solutions to the problem.

After you assess your culture, a total reset or partial adjustment is often necessary. Dr. Chand noted the dangers of failing to address or change cultures that are toxic or passive. These produce inferior products; the brand is unreliable and no longer relevant. How often do we accept inferior contributions from long-term associates, friends, workers, or even volunteers?

Changing a brand is a laborious effort. It is slow but necessary in our personal lives. The corporate or professional culture is the sum total of our individual contributions. *After* thinkers are willing to establish a brand free from known adversities. One of the greatest challenges in life is taking a risk to leave what's familiar and strike out into the unknown. This is your moment to dare to be different. Today is your opportunity to reach out to people in your community who inspire you to be your best. Now is the time to create that connection with a potential mentor who could help you take your vision for life to the next level.

Are your current friends or associates motivational or fearful? Are they adventurers or complacent? There's no way to have a successful *after* without the right people fueling your present, your future, and your legacy. You may not be able to make an immediate geographical relocation, but you can start to shift the types of conversations you are having. Associates influence our lives and futures. As you begin to focus your thoughts toward what comes next, your life will begin to be a reflection of your God-given destiny.

Division of Labor

Division of labor is critical to branding. "And we beseech you, brethren, to know them that labor among you, and are over you in the Lord, and admonish you" (1 Thessalonians 5:12 KJV). This exercise will help you divide the labor required in your *after* and evaluate the people on your team.

List every person who has been an essential part of your life in the last six months. On a scale of 1–10, 1 being the worst and 10 being the best, rate each person based on their contributions to your life.

Do you have life-affirming conversations with this person? Are they coming to you with substantive value or waste? Are they interested in helping you to further your goals and dreams? Are they only interested in keeping you mired in negativity?

_____

_____

_____

_____

_____

_____

_____

_____

_____

Now that you have rated each person, you can decide who gets to join you for which celebration. I have no problem inviting 1s, 2s, or 3s to join me in the park for a cupcake or a burger. They can have all the cupcakes they want. But 1s, 2s, and 3s have no business sitting giving input to a new brand.

Letting go is a very difficult task not because of performance measures but because of loyalty and the power of culture. Rewarding loyalty for poor behavior is similar to feeding a poisonous snake. You feed him from gestation to adulthood, but he will certainly give you the bite of death when you are no longer able to provide.

One of my worst professional mistakes was rehiring a former engineer who was hungry and homeless and bringing him into my inner circle. He was not inspirational or supportive. Not only was he detrimental to my business, but he betrayed me, giving confidential information to competitors that severely cut into my profits and damaged my brand. Protect and value that which has been given to you. Teaching others does not include giving others the keys and codes to your treasures when they are less than loyal and dedicated to your brand.

—— ❁ ——

Becoming a Powerful Brand

Money and people are cyclical resources. In business, I've found that there are times when you have money, and that attracts people to the business. Conversely, there are times when you have little money, causing people to depart as resources decline. But *after* establishes brand loyalty, which remains stable while individuals, funds, or both vacillate. This kind of branding looks inward to attract new relationships and find untapped resources. Never allow yourself to become extinct; remember, your brand is powerful!

My mother, with a limited formal education, became a brand herself. Years after her death, she remains relevant beyond her immediate family. Betty Loyd was a brand unto herself. My mother's brand was symbolic of excellence, push, desire, a thirst for knowledge, and zero tolerance for failure. She was an avid reader who never finished high school, a great speaker, wise mother, landowner, and businesswoman. Her brand was solid without monetary means or a high school diploma. Education is essential to obtaining your brand. Nevertheless, some of your best lessons will come from pain instead of lectures or coursework.

Believe it or not, pain and resistance can leave you in a stronger position. Anyone who does anything worthwhile will face opposition, but it can be like weight training; the more resistance, the stronger the muscles become. As a leader, entrepreneur, and certified executive-level life coach, it's not uncommon for me to meet opposition while in pursuit of expanding dreams and passions. As you lead your brand, prepare for opposition.

As Albert Einstein said, "Great spirits have always encountered violent opposition from mediocre minds."[7] Orison Swett Marden tells us, "Success is not measured by what you accomplish, but by the opposition you have encountered, and the courage with which you have maintained the struggle against overwhelming odds."

Thomas Rainer, in a lecture, gave this insightful definition regarding leadership: "Leadership without opposition is perhaps following others." The adverse moments of life often affect leaders, or what I like to call "Dream Walkers," in a particular way. Leaders often lack moral support, and they face heightened risks. Others often desire the benefit of success without paying the price of loyalty, commitment, and trustworthiness, placing the burden on the leader. Sharing our struggles as leaders is often taken as a sign of defeat and weakness. Great leaders are not weak; they often attract opposition because of their forthcoming victory. Our mental battles far outweigh physical encounters. Your "purpose" drives you into reaching for more while others are reaching to end your pursuit. Success is a battle that few understand and many will encounter.

As you act effectively as the leader and manager of your new personal brand, you'll find that having dreams and aspirations never comes without external opposition. But opposition should never reduce one into an oppressed state of mind—where we give up or let circumstances stop us from looking toward the future with creativity. To that end, let's amend our definition of real power to include money, resources, and people, plus internal *determination*. Determination will often precede acquiring money, resources, or people, and it will supersede the loss of them.

Think back to Maslow's pyramid of self-actualization discussed in the last chapter. Lack, change, or shatterings in one level of the pyramid can keep you from rising to the top or hinder you from succeeding, and ultimately interrupt the joy of self-actualization. Determination must become your best friend. It must become your trademark. Determination is what makes a powerful brand.

Evaluate Your Brand

Let's give life to your brand creation. What symbolizes your image or your power? When people hear your name, what image is established without speaking? Do they say, *strong, resilient, determined, trustworthy, a person of integrity*? What is synonymous with your presence? How can you become so valuable and indispensable in the marketplace of life that you, like Hostess' Twinkie, have the "sweetest comeback ever"? There's an art to becoming a successful brand. On one block in LA near USC's campus, a doughnut shop, a Starbucks, and a McDonalds appear in close quarters. Starbucks and the Golden Arches compete to attract customers for the coffee needed to accompany the doughnut. Cost is not a factor in branding. The only thing that matters here is that these two powerful companies have made a compelling desire for their products.

After branding suggests your value is beyond one entity or consumer. "One man's trash is another man's treasure." Branding does not seek to undermine or confront another; neither does it claim defeat when another arises. Healthy economies are birthed from choices. I have gift cards to both Starbucks and McDonalds; the product is coffee but the brand is distinctly different. What is the critical message? Coffee is a great compliment to doughnuts. Starbucks and McDonalds realized their brands go well with this small, family-owned doughnut shop. Neither try to make doughnuts but rather serve the best coffee as a compliment. Your brand has value and should be placed where it is respected and provides a compliment to others.

Make time to evaluate your brand—whether it's effective, whether it connects to people, and whether it complements them. You must know what works and what needs to be removed. Evaluate your gains and losses by setting a tone and value. Start your rebranding with relevant questions, such as:

1. What happens if I do nothing, if I don't rebrand?

2. How will I feel if deliberate changes are made?

3. When do I wish to start this process?

4. Whom can I trust?

5. What are the core values of my brand?

6. Who will benefit most from my brand? What "customer need" could my brand serve?

7. Where will my resources come from?

8. Who will I allow to be on my team, and who could be toxic to the brand I want to build?

This is the moment to assess who is surrounding your destiny and redefine your culture. Resetting or rebranding life is not an easy endeavor. Establishing a brand is never casually achieved. But with the key ingredients of resources (internal and external), people, perspective, and determination, you can position your personal brand to make the "sweetest comeback ever."

Reflection Questions

1. Think of a powerful personal brand of someone you admire. What aspects make that brand powerful to you?

_____

_____

_____

2. What are the hallmarks of the brand you wish to build?

_____

_____

_____

3. What is the purpose of your brand?

_____

_____

_____

4. How does your relationship to monetary resources hinder or help you? How could determination and creativity change that relationship?

    _____

    _____

    _____

5. What did you learn from the exercise in dividing the labor in your life, or evaluating the people on your branding team?

    _____

    _____

    _____

6. How have you seen a poverty mind-set in action in your life? What kind of mind-set is its antidote?

    _____

    _____

    _____

7. How can you prepare for opposition in your branding?

    _____

    _____

    _____

CHAPTER 9

Sustainability

We wish each other well. We chalk misfortunes up to chance, failing to consider our contributions to these events. Your *after* is not based upon luck or chance. It requires the work described in this book as well as action.

What is luck or chance? It's a house without a foundation.

Countless people enter casinos or purchase lottery tickets hoping "lady luck" or good fortune will arrive. But the ratio of losing versus winning is staggering. Even for those who do win, their "luck" often doesn't last. Lottery winners seldom record sustainable wealth after winning. When luck gives a win, it often takes a much bigger loss.

No, *after* is not found by luck or some abstract force causing good things to occur. It comes by giving deliberate attention to causing positive change in our lives. Leaving things to chance is a gamble or an attempt to beat the odds. Relying on chance can lead to addictions with costly effects. Instead of chance, focus on change—the kind of change that leads to sustainable stability in your future, both morally and financially. Change is not luck; it is sustainable behavior producing exponential benefit over a period of time.

Sustainable success can seem like a far-off dream when we find ourselves facing shattered lives. We can become lethargic, fearful of the obstacles that stand in the way of sustainable success. Paul reminds us, however, "We wrestle not against flesh and blood but against principalities" (Ephesians 6:12 KJV). Sustainable success is available when life's obstructions causes one to trip or fall. The process is simple; pick yourself up and continue the pursuit of life.

Principalities are essential abstract beings, thoughts, or behaviors found inside our culture or being. These are timeless elements that seek to override progress while seeking to formulate thoughts of failure or fuel fear that leads into captivity. Our drive toward *after* requires us to war against these things. Principalities seek to bring us back into forms of captivity and undermine our pursuit of *after* or the sustainable joyful position of life. As Paul reminds us, we must wrestle against them. It is no luck of the draw to win against these principalities; it is a wrestling match.

Even in the face of failure, even when we've fallen down, sustainable success is still available while getting up is possible. *After* does not accept failure. It actively promotes the future and seeks to find sponsorship, never operating in "lucky" mind-sets. Believers must live with transformative mind-sets and practice behavior modifications that lead to sustainable success. No matter what situation we find ourselves in, we must believe that our lives are rich with new, sustainable opportunities.

What Is Success?

What does *success* mean to you? The word certainly means different things to different people. And each person has an exclusive right to define his or her success model. If we let social norms or appearances dictate our definition of success, we get nowhere. Outward expressions of success are overrated, and they create false narratives in life.

Think back to our discussion of branding in the previous chapter. Luxury brands and labels flood today's marketplace, creating imagery along with symbolism, from Mercedes to Luis Vuitton to Apple.

Brand managers seek consumers by design and sophisticated marketing, hoping they will connect a sense of success with their label. Purchasing a product does not give consumers sustained success, but the power of messaging creates a narrative that this person is successful because they have this product. Material acquisitions do not define success. Wealth often travels in a light pick-up truck instead of a luxury car or chooses to sleep in a motel versus a five-star hotel. Let's be clear, theirs is a matter of choice but not a limit of funds. We all know individuals who possess material imagery but lack financial stability. *After* helps you reset values and establish a means to sustain life, avoiding debt and depression. The perception of success is vastly different than authentic, sustainable success. *After* provides platforms for sustained success beyond a label.

Once you have defined your brand, you must define what it means to be a successful brand—a sustainable brand. This starts by comparing yourself today to the self you see in your future. What are your goals and objectives in five or ten years from today? Have you listed strategic and tactical goals for your life? Or have you become distracted with the mere garments or labels of success?

Sustainable success requires eliminating distractions or concepts that darken your focus. Gambling may not be your weakness, or conspicuous consumerism may not be your problem, but let's be clear: most people who see sustained success have had to make behavior modifications to remain successful. They have had to stop doing things that don't lead to success, and adopt new practices that help them flourish.

Success is desired globally, but rarely acquired because it requires process, planning, and sacrifice. Success is a holistic state of being, and it goes beyond external, obvious monetary elements. Success encompasses our mind, body, and soul.

How does one then achieve success? Once you define what success means to you, you embark on behavior modifications that bring you closer to your goal.

Sustainable Behavior Modifications

Consider your brand. What one word best describes what you want your brand perception to be? Branding yourself in this way can change your mind-set, producing stability and removing prevailing images of failure or surrender. The Ritz Carlton brand suggests superior customer service, name recognition, and luxurious amenities. The Ritz has a sustainable image because it is strong, simple, and based on repeatable excellence. *The Five Star Church* was written to bring this quality mind-set, foundational to the Ritz Carlton's culture, to the church.[8] A five-star establishment will train, train, and retrain all employees to bring excellence from point of entry until departure. This is the kind of behavior modification that works to produce sustainable success.

Why not rebuild life around your desired image, net worth, and victorious return? What one word best describes your intended success? "*I am* _____." Now, what repeated action can bring you closer to it? How can you "retrain" yourself to reach it?

Sustainable strength is the sum total of mind, body, and soul. It requires more than one trip to the fitness center or a single bike ride; it requires consistent behavior modification. Unfortunately, building a new, sustainable you often requires a release of the old and obtaining something new. We are so addicted to old behaviors that change becomes difficult.

Diabetes is common in my family, so it's been one of my life's goals to avoid foods that contribute to this disease. My desire for fried food is gone, easily dismissed. My desire for chocolate is dead, as is my desire for soda. I eat egg whites, oatmeal, and spinach, drink water, and exercise, but giving up gourmet jellybeans seemed like the most difficult task in the world. I would spend hours exercising, walking, and riding a bike only to sit down with a book and read with a bowl of exotic flavored jelly beans. Mango, pineapple, cherry burst, and apple crisp—once I started, it was hard to stop. When my glucose numbers hit the roof, so did my doctor. She asked what I was doing differently. Truthfully, I had given up some things but not enough to rebuild my health. I had to forever say goodbye to gourmet jelly beans to save my life and to rebuild my mind, body, and spirit. Behavior modification, even in seemingly small areas, can add up to make a sustainable transformation.

Psychologist and behaviorist B. F. Skinner pioneered research on behavior modification theory in the 1940s and 50s. He explored which methods produced desired outcomes through modified behaviors. Skinner suggested sustainable outcomes—lasting positive changes—were more likely when positive affirmations or actions were reinforced. Changes in our lives are not acts of random luck or a lottery system. Sustainable changes in life occur through behavior modification and reinforcement. Your *after* will require you to make modifications that will result in lasting positive change.

Saying goodbye to gourmet jelly beans may seem like a minor feat compared to other addictions in life. Remember: small amounts of toxicity will destroy your life. The size or sugar content of one jelly bean is negligible—until you begin ingesting one every hour for six years. Our lives are seldom destroyed immediately through small amounts of negativity, but meager beginnings can produce fatal results over time.

Positive reinforcement displaces the bad and replaces it with good. Positive replacements are never immediate but occur through deliberate, disciplined channels of change. Prayer is a priceless asset to positive reinforcement. Giving to others is another form of positive reinforcement. Trust is a major form of positive reinforcement; although slow, the process is certain to produce positive results.

What behaviors are you repeating that take you where you do not want to be? Scripture advises us: "Let us examine our ways and test them, and let us return to the Lord" (Lamentations 3:40 NIV). Your "ways," or daily habits and behaviors, all add up. Spend the next few days or weeks keeping track of what you spend your time doing. Then ask yourself if any of those behaviors are detracting from the goal you set for yourself, for your brand, or for your life. Do not waste time by putting undue hope in "luck" or outside forces. Undoing these behaviors will be hard, but it's not impossible. You can let go and move forward.

Lasting Change in Communities

Building a new you is critical following a season of shattering, whether from unforeseen medical challenges, ministry upheavals, marital meltdowns, divorce, cancer, betrayal, loss of life, loss of employment, loss of business, or simply the loss of desire. It is just as important on a community level as it is on an individual level.

From 2016 through the present we have seen an upsurge of unrest in many domestic communities. Governmental issues are impacting communities as injustice and inequalities remain. Evangelicals are fighting with religious leaders, while families are being torn apart through political agendas. School shootings are as common as the sun rising and shining, while some turn deaf ears to these communities. Is there an *after* for our communities, cities, and nation?

The unrest shows no signs of stopping. We find ourselves wondering if it is unsafe to go into movie theaters, or even to go into a church in South Carolina. Unrest has ramped up within our society, including economic unrest among millennials, who face staggering unemployment rates within their age group. Adding to the instability, a recent Supreme Court ruling found overcrowding in prisons to be unconstitutional and granted paroles to nearly 30,000 inmates in California. This reentry process presents socioeconomic challenges for urban communities with minimal employment opportunities and health care. The need to build a life *after* is real and immediate.

As we think about a sustainable future for ourselves, we must bring this thinking into our communities. Public policy, tools, conversations, plans, and general care are needed to accomplish this. Sustainability through stable contributions is critical to building safe, caring communities and public policy.

After brings a sense of accountability or awareness to your social, spiritual, and economical surroundings. The question should transition from "Who is doing something?" to "What needs to be changed or added to turn hopelessness into hope or failures into success?" The local family, church, schools, and communities are positioned for contribution. Nothing worth having is easy or achieved without sacrifice, time, and patience. *After* seekers find themselves making consistent small contributions, not for self-glory or position, but to give life to others.

Warren Buffet is a great donor to philanthropic causes; he believes giving is the greatest gift to receive. Monetary contributions are great, but in the absence of money, your new you at a school or AA meeting or community center for children is a form of returning life to underserved communities. Your local church can be blessed when you give your time. This benevolence is priceless, and its fosters new life and light where failure or darkness prevailed.

We must be committed to solutions, both on a public and private level. It's easy to be overcome by a terrible state of affairs. Are you inspired to move toward a better future, or do you feel a need to express additional traumas?

A single mother with a simple, powerful, sometimes insensitive but always loving message set my experience model. My mother, Betty, had a philosophy for life, which was simply, "It happened, it hurt, and it was real. Let's talk, heal, and move on."

My mother lived in an *after* state of mind without knowing it. She insisted upon resolutions instead of excuses. She knew we had more value in our future than in the residue of our past. Most great innovative minds experience pain, disappointments, and pressures on the way to their goals. But this is valuable; if we became free of pain or disappointments, our abilities would become self-centered, creating a false sense of worth. A life void of pain and disappointment suggests you are perfect in your own right. Pain pushes you into a vulnerable need, even if it's back into the voice of your mother. A voice that tells us to rebuild.

Rebuilding

When the World Trade Center collapsed, great sorrow and pain washed over not only America, but the world. I recently visited the World Trade Center Memorial in New York and saw countless relics from that devastating moment. Yet, there was no way to avoid seeing new life and construction rising in the same area of destruction. Building replaces pain. It never erases the past, but it brings light and life to your future.

Resetting one's aspirations is never an easy task. Many choose to remain stuck instead of obtaining tools to regain confidence and character, and taking corrective measures. America became a greater nation following 9/11, but only for a moment. We now have become riddled with internal hatred, bigotry, police brutality, and contentious political values.

From this we must learn a key principle: sustainable rebuilding starts with a *cause*, not from a crisis. Though you may have been through a crisis, personally or as a community, the way forward will be powered by a cause. Let your cause, not a crisis, be the fuel for sustainable positive change. Let your cause fuel your contribution.

If you are seeking value in your *after*, there will be risks and opposition. Building anything of value requires confronting and mitigating risks. Staying down is safe, but is it rewarding? Doing nothing is safe, but is it fulfilling? Perhaps we take fewer risks as we age in life; this is understandable, but should not be acceptable. Life is not valued in time alone, but it is measured by events and impressions left upon those who would otherwise remain unchanged if it were not for your contributions.

Build on Your Value

Know your value. These three words are so relevant when building an authentic and sustainable future. But how can we describe value in real terms? Net worth signifies value in assets minus liabilities. Knowing your personal value comes from making an internal inspection of who you are. Are you a born leader or a trained leader? Having knowledge of your leadership qualities and attributes is not enough. You have to remain on the course even when hope is gone, health is challenged, marriage is muddy, or associates betray you. Your real net worth begins with knowing who you are and having a keen sense of your abilities and accomplishments.

Let's be bold and list the things you have set in motion. You are a great creation formed by the Almighty to accomplish greater works following horrific upheavals of life. It is now your time to build momentum.

I became a certified executive-level life coach so I could help activate momentum and pride among great leaders who have fallen prey to the cares of this life. As one who has crossed many professional and public thresholds alone, I knew that feeling of being overwhelmed was normal while pursuing a new cause or vision. I recall asking my peers how best to handle a critical care matter when my wife was diagnosed with stage-four cancer two weeks before our wedding. Prominent men in my circle pushed away from the question and my presence. I was left alone to walk through a maze of life that I would never wish on another man or woman. In this time I realized that sometimes the greatest possible resource is not monetary, but spiritual support with a measure of compassion. Looking back it's clear; *after* is my answer to how to handle critical care, to continue with life, and to find sustainable strength by building a new you. And calculating your value is key to sustainability.

I have found that professional or personal building is a three-part process, similar to the three parts of this book. You may find other effective methods, but to reach *after*, it is vital to have a plan and process in place. Let's unpack these methods and bring structure to your rebuilding process:

Leaving Your Past

- Conduct internal and external evaluations

- Remove unwanted barriers of mistrust

- Remember the power of forgiveness

- Eliminate toxic powers of unforgiveness

- Create a new formula

  » Accept those things you cannot change

  » Leave those things that prohibit your positive change

  » Push into those things that define you

Exploration

- Redefine your purpose for your life (branding)

- Revamp right relationships

- Define critical factors you will need to move forward:

  » Family, finance, and friends

  » Networking with critical contributors

  » Establishing outcomes and impacts

Execution

- Execute a plan to make a difference in your life

- Be realistic; shattering was a process, and so is building

- Find a coach and be held accountable

Building a new you is so vital to the sustainable success of your *after*. Find partners who possess like interests, and embrace new territory and events in life. I have found that two specific personality tests can assist in this building a new you, pointing out your strengths and your value.

The first is called Enneagram, which you can discover at www.enneagraminstitute.com. The second is Strengths Finder, which you can find in a printed book (*StrengthsFinder 2.0* by Tom Rath) and online at www.gallupstrengthscenter.com. These two resources will assist you in the evaluation process.

Lastly, become accountable to someone or a group who will propel you into building a new you. Accountability is effective only when the partner knows your goals and objectives.

With these tools, you can build on your value, make lasting change, and reap the rewards of behavior modification. The time is right for finding a sustainable, stable *after*.

Reflection Questions

1. Have you found yourself relying on luck in the past? How can a change in mind-set set you up for a more sustainable future?

_____

_____

_____

2. Beyond money, what defines success for you?

_____

_____

3. What small behaviors might be adding up to keep you from success?

_____

_____

_____

4. What behavior modifications could replace them, using positive reinforcement?

    _____

    _____

    _____

5. In what ways have you seen positive behavior modifications work in the past?

    _____

    _____

    _____

6. How can you contribute to lasting change in your community?

    _____

    _____

    _____

7. Reflect on your "value." How can you know your value more thoroughly, and what steps will you take to build on that value?

    _____

    _____

    _____

CHAPTER 10

Building Capacity

D o you remember waiting patiently to receive a Sears catalogue to do your Christmas shopping at home, phone in hand? The current generation has no concept of this relic. Those catalogue days are over. Google, Amazon, and online retailers have risen to take the market share. It all comes down to the idea of capacity. A consumer depends upon suppliers to have sufficient inventory and logistical support to meet their needs—and quickly. A market must meet consumer demand or suffer severe consequences, including bankruptcy or extinction. Sears, Kmart, and JC Penney are losing market shares because they lack capacity to meet today's consumer trends. Online retailers, however, have capacity to serve a seemingly infinite number of consumers.

Ministry as we knew it has also undergone enormous cultural and sociological changes due to our consumer culture. The impacts are vast in our communities; family values have shifted, core values for life have moved from sharing to selfishness. Additionally, mass numbers see little or no value in the local church while it struggles to remain valuable and relevant. Sears is closing hundreds of its stores along with other chain retailers. Why? Their capacity to service change was underestimated, as were methods to evaluate a declining interest in standard practices. Hence the arrival of Amazon, and other electronic mediums which have underscored the ethics of capacity.

As our personal worlds change, we must build our own capacity to remain relevant, productive, desired, and profitable in our *after.* Paul, in 1 Corinthians 12:4–14, speaks of gifts we are given in the body of Christ, with the understanding that we all have the ability to build capacity when led by the Spirit.

In building capacity, we prepare for expansion. It is the process of developing and strengthening the skills, instincts, resources, abilities, and external contributions required to thrive in your *after*. Part of capacity building is removing unwanted barriers. It is replacing empty channels in life with ones that lead to opportunities. Capacity building follows picking up the pieces and branding; it involves defined planning to never repeat history.

Capacity building was the backbone of Reverend Dr. Cecil Murray USC Center For Community Engagement lectures. Dr. Murray has made enormous contributions to social and religious efforts spanning nearly four decades in Southern California. His literary work *Twice Tested by Fire* gives epic insights to his life journey and solidifies him as an expert in capacity building. According to Dr. Murray, capacity defines both a man and his culture. Capacity speaks to our future drive, developmental objectives, and determination.

Once value is established, the need to define capacity is necessary and critical. How can you obtain greatness without knowing your value? This chapter is dedicated to building your sustainable powers and revealing your value. We will transcend norms of thinking and enlarge our apertures to see life as people who have overcome history and now possess dreams.

Capacity and Progress

Capacity measures your ability to successfully manage a variety of tasks simultaneously. And *progress* is a move forward. This definition is so simple it has become complicated. Progress and failure never occur at a one-to-one ratio. Ten years of failure can be undone with one day of success. One open door or a single success will erase years of loss and pain. Are you able and willing to amass exponential success? Is your structure and team strategically ready for the phenomenal opportunity? Do you have the capacity to take on new expanding territories? What is required to reach this level?

To build capacity, you must take critical inventory of your current ability. You look at the gaps, asking what is within your ability and what remains beyond it. Who has what is needed, and where are they? These steps will determine your current capacity and help you identify missing shareholders or contributions required to support an expanding model. Whatever your expanding model might be—success in building a strong marriage or family, building your career, building your wisdom and knowledge, building a circle of deep friendships, building your faith into a powerful force for good—prepare to enlarge your capacity.

Think of capacity as a light switch. A sensor or light switch has capacity to control a vast electrical current. We never see electricity, but one switch can provide light to an enormous facility. Light and life move at similar speeds. We need a switch to help us manage the current, and that switch is our capacity—having systems in place to control raw power through systematic order.

Perhaps your life was once unregulated, boring, or mundane. Or perhaps it was unreasonably chaotic or reeling from shattering events. But today there's a spark within your being and thoughts. You are rebuilding hope of the "sweet comeback" we discussed in a previous chapter. That hope—that comeback—is an asset. And it is worth protecting. We must build from our mistakes and establish a credible, uplifting future. We must make progress. Others will become attracted to your dreams and ideas; these cast a great presence in your community, among your peers. So how are you going to manage this new season of life? What is your plan for success? You must build capacity!

Capacity for the Unexpected

Unexpected events are part of life. To reach your *after*, you must prepare for the unexpected. You must be ready to navigate through uncharted waters. Google Maps do not exist for this journey. Siri lacks the content or capacity to process the unexpected—and you will encounter the unexpected. *After* requires adjustment of old norms or ideas when your best-laid plans do not materialize. Success may be interrupted by events inside or outside of our control. How do we react when after years of study and professional success, we hear the words, "It's cancer"? How does one cope when dreams materialize then evaporate due to fiscal or unforeseen events?

Our Creator desires total trust throughout the progression of life, and He commands the universe knowing some will and some will not trust Him. Trusting Him is an activity called faith. Faith simply means having obtained the ability to trust while in unexpected storms of life, business, ministry, or simple dreams. Our life's concerns are proving grounds, teaching us to make plans to succeed when the unexpected occurs.

Taking control of your life is possible, but it must be deliberate, with a rhythm of consistent direction and purpose. Success building calls for extensive commitment. Capacity is not the mere size of your gas tank; it is made up of a number of elements, including one's ability to reach beyond their immediate resources and collaborate with others creating a partnership of strength. It is gathering additional resources so as not to limit or destroy our vision or dream. We are often limited by our own inability to build viable relationships outside of our immediate area. But as you build capacity, you will find resources beyond your "normal." Commitment alone is no guarantee of success, unless there is value and positive attention given to your *people*, your *purpose*, and your *plan*.

Your People: Know Your True Friends

There's an old adage that says, "You will know your true friends when the unexpected arrives." Knowing your true friends is effectively evaluating the capacity of your relationships. Placing too much value on unhealthy or unproven external relationships prior to an unexpected season of life is perhaps the most misguided, underestimated, devastating mistake one can make. Who in your circle has the capacity to keep confidence with you when you face the unexpected?

Dr. Samuel Chand credits his relationship with God, his wife, and his internal fortitude for his success. He pastored more than three thousand church members, yet he admitted he found himself with a smaller circle of true supporters during his unexpected moments.[9] Rick Warren, noted author, motivational speaker, and megachurch leader, also found himself recently grappling with unexpected moments, in need of support from a small group of people. One of my close personal friends, who also pastored a megachurch, recently shared how troubled he had become over feeling unsafe inside the circle of his peers. As he shared his internal struggles, I leaned toward him and asked, "Why do you feel safe sharing this with me?" He replied, "Because you have never repeated whatever I have said to you outside of this place." Later that week, he had a massive heart attack on a plane with his wife at his side. I did not know this would be our last meal together. What a great compliment to know that he felt safe with me until his death. I will take those private moments with him to my grave. My greatest contribution was providing him with a safe place.

We must work at building our safe place and being that safe place for others. Many people are facing increasing levels of mistrust within their circle of peers. Peer-to-peer breakdowns in business sectors are equally as destructive as those in religious circles, which lead to declines in church membership and conflict in church leadership.

The distance between peers is counterproductive as we seek to build volume, life success, or even church membership without understanding the principle of capacity in our trusting relationships. I have seen several prominent leaders vacating influential pulpits due to interpersonal challenges. This wasn't due to fiscal or practical matters, but having inept preparation for success. This leads back to capacity.

A business associate coined the hashtag #DiTD, or "doing one thing differently," as a means to offer productive alternatives where poor choices, inappropriate decisions, and disappointment seem to rule the day. You may have to DiTD in your relationships. It's vitally important to evaluate the moral fiber of your inner circle. Find partnerships with shared values and common ground. Partners may disagree, and healthy confrontation is profitable when it promotes capacity.

Capacity is not the size of your facility but the strength of your mind-set. How does one build capacity? It involves accepting a need for evaluation. It involves assessing one's interpersonal aptitude. Become concerned without being overly critical of past decisions. Observe the good, realizing great is better than good. List the failures and faults in your endeavors, and find out whether they are due to internal problems or external problems. A professional counselor once provided me a critical lesson on building capacity following a catastrophe: We make decisions based on perception versus knowledge. Never hold yourself accountable for the misrepresentations of others.

The Loyalty Code

California, like many other states, periodically deals with organized gang activity. Political unrest stemming from our recent elections has shifted the media's attention away from the problem, but the scourge of gang violence continues.

One of my current staff members is a former gang member. He recently shared his unique perspective in our ministry circle. He outlined for us the ethics and codes within gangs, noting how they set territory and upheld internal respect within these guidelines.

He then explained the art of protection and of protecting vital information from rival gangs. In short, he said, "We covered one another." Ethical codes inside gangs hinge upon basic tenants: never reveal insider information to outsiders, never question a direction, and remain loyal to the code and not the situation. An ethical code is essential in establishing capacity. I want to be clear: in no way do I endorse, condone, or promote gang violence. I do not believe in the ethics that underlie it. But we can observe that the strength of these gangs lies in loyalty; their expansion relies on organized codes. There is no question—they do incalculable harm in our communities; yet, they draw strength from a principle that we cannot and should not ignore if we are going to build capacity for good in our lives. What gangs have used for evil, we must reclaim for good. We must learn to cover one another. Using godly principles, in a spirit of love, reflect on what true respect means to you and what you want to nurture in your community. Build a better culture of trust within your circles. Know your true friends, and be a true friend.

Your Purpose

As it is with many aspects of *after,* understanding your purpose is critical as you build your capacity. Again, we can draw from the world of business to find that understanding.

Capacity building in my aerospace company was strategic. E & I Systems' purpose went beyond providing software tests and evaluation support to the Federal Aviation Administration. Our purpose was to champion new opportunities and offer careers to those brilliant engineers, analysts, and support workers who may never be hired by a *Fortune* 500 corporation.

I was able to gain priceless tools while working in a *Fortune* 500 firm knowing some were transferable and others were embedded in that culture. Our corporate goals at E & I were strategic and built around relationships and some competition. Competition is healthy to sustained success in today's marketplace and ministry. We measured our capacity for growth in static goals, we compared them with our competitors', and we made growth projections. We used both known and unknown variables in making those projections.

In life, our capacity is never based upon known variables, but rather unknown variables. These are the unthinkable, unplanned, unprepared for, unimaginable, unrecoverable, undesirable, unforgiveable, and ungodly moments.

Unexpected Growth

My capacity-building moment in life occurred between 2008 and 2015. Conversely, my business, E & I Systems, built capacity in a mere thirty-six months, making us ready to accept exponential growth in a highly competitive aerospace industry. It is often easier to build capacity with structured business models than within our circle of relationships. While America was undergoing a financial meltdown, my personal life and business life underwent its worst season, and I was battered by unexpected, painful events. During this season, I recall visiting my then critically ill mother, who asked me, "What are you obtaining from this season of life?" She never asked, "*Why* are you going through this?" She did not ask *why,* but *what.* Pain, in this case, was a teacher. She reminded me that expanding often results in pain, and must always contend with pain, either from within or without.

I never thought pain produced value until this season of unexpected outcomes reached epic proportions. I returned to Mother with this answer to her question, which remains constant in my life: I learned to never over-personalize the outcomes, but learn that some are outside of your control and decision-making processes. *After* does not seek to know why events occur but understands the prime value is in asking what is gained through the event.

To build capacity in business requires examination of known deficiencies, then bringing additional resources to areas in need. I have built businesses to capacity in short periods of time, yet doing this in other sectors of life is another matter entirely. Purpose is built with pain. Pain contributes to capacity. Once pain shows us our areas of weakness, we can take steps to strengthen those areas. Rebuilding after a disaster, whether conceptual or real, is painful but extremely beneficial now that the storm has passed.

Your Plan for Capacity

My best friend Dr. G and I continued to meet regularly and encourage each other up until his untimely death. We had a monthly plan in place. We had committed to being open and honest—to sustaining each other. We knew we each had a great deal of pain to learn from in building capacity. He encouraged me, and I encouraged him. We never condemned one another's unexpected moments or allowed each other to become victims. Dr. G was never critical of my personal life; neither did he point out my faults or failures. We had a mutual respect for life and the perils of leadership, ministry, family, finance, and relationships. We began building capacity with a plan and knowing we had to find what came next in both of our lives.

He wanted to build a medical facility, while others thought it was impossible and lacked adequate support. Dr. G and I met regularly to reinforce one another and give moral support, knowing this level of encouragement exceeded monetary contributions. Regular support and planning is essential while building capacity.

A brilliant chapter in Malcolm Gladwell's book *Outliers* describes how masters at their craft become prepared for their big break. He uses the example of the Beatles and the nearly ten thousand hours they played in local bars in England in the early 60s before rising to fame. When it came time for them to take on their first record deal, they were well prepared to step into their moment because they had been giving their all for years before anyone knew of John, Paul, George, or Ringo. Their legendary British Invasion in America was not due to a far-off dream of a plan, but a real plan backed up with real effort and real support.[10] We must become dedicated, purposeful, and true to the plan to build capacity.

In your *after*, there is no such thing as an instant overnight success. In the movie *Straight Outta Compton*, we observe the plan that N.W.A. used to create their success as one of the most influential groups in hip hop history. They developed a sense of independence and wealth from severe social pain. They began building capacity from small gigs into enormous arenas. Today, founding member Dr. Dre's headphone company was recently purchased by Apple, making him even more wealthy with a sound brand. We can learn much from this in ministry circles and in our personal lives. N.W.A. had the ability to get beyond differences, splits, and internal death to create a global external brand largely because they knew how to build capacity.

Build Capacity with Words

"Death and life are in the power of the tongue" (Proverbs 18:21). This is both amazing and terrifying. The mouth can give birth to a vision or kill your possibilities. We live in an unforgiving society. We must build capacity with deliberate self-preserving statements. We must become purposeful builders for our *after* today.

To do this, guard your thoughts and your tongue. Be wary of destructive thoughts and statements such as:

- I am not smart enough to do that.

- I will never be successful.

- I cannot please my father or mother.

- That might be good for some, but I know it doesn't work for me.

- At this age, it's impossible.

Positive meditation and positive speech, however, can expand your capacity. It can give birth to inspiration and positive action. Repeat:

- I will be successful.

- I must not seek to please others who are unfulfilled.

- Life is never over until death comes.

- Time is of the essence.

- What I lack, others will provide.

- I am not afraid of success.

- My mind is greater than my money.

- Great minds attract wealthy donors.

- Life begins when you dare to dream again.

Our most finite commodity is time. Do not waste it regretting the past or bemoaning your circumstances. Find relationships that enhance your model and increase your capacity to create a new you, with endless possibilities.

In summary, remember these basic principles to build your capacity:

1. Identify your trustworthy inner circle

2. Build trusting capacity in your relationships

3. Review your purpose

4. Identify your weaknesses and areas of pain that keep you from growing

5. Address each area of weakness by making a plan and bringing in resources

6. Identify what you need to do to be prepared for your big break

7. Continue taking small steps toward success, making a long-term plan

8. Remember that failure does not define capacity; that was an isolated event in time

9. Follow your heart; listen to your future, not your failures

10. Expand your thoughts—capacity will follow

Reflection Questions

1. Do you believe you currently have the capacity to reach your idea of success? If not, where do you need to build capacity?

    _____

    _____

    _____

2. In reaching your goals, what is within your ability? What is beyond it?

    _____

    _____

    _____

3. What resources can you bring in to help you attain what is beyond your ability?

    _____

    _____

    _____

4. Identify five markers of progress that would represent a move forward in your capacity. What steps can you take to come closer to these goals?

   _____

   _____

   _____

5. Strategize: What unexpected events might prevent you from reaching your goals or expanding capacity? How would you respond?

   _____

   _____

   _____

6. How does reviewing your people, your purpose, and your plan help you build capacity?

   _____

   _____

   _____

7. What words of life will you speak over yourself as you build?

   _____

   _____

   _____

PART 3

Pressing Onward Toward the Goal

*Brothers and sisters, I do not consider myself yet to have taken hold of it. But one thing I do: Forgetting what is behind and straining toward what is ahead, I **press on toward the goal** to win the prize for which God has called me heavenward in Christ Jesus.*

Philippians 3:13–14 NIV

CHAPTER 11

From Limping to Running

An infant begins walking between nine months and one year of age. I have mentioned that when I was a child, a disease affecting bone structure—rickets—stunted this season of my life, leaving me incapacitated until three years of age. Early childhood development is essential to building a healthy and strong adult. Anyone who has experienced childhood adversity knows that the effects can linger far into adulthood, in social, emotional, or physical impairments. Some never lose post-traumatic symptoms and scarring, physical or mental, developed while in this period. In fact, a recent study in the *Journal of the American Medical Association* shows that "early childhood adversity … may carry heavy consequences from generation to generation."[11] But what if we were to view this adversity not as a curse, but as a source of strength?

I have a priceless black-and-white photo of my two-year-old self with my father just before his illness and death. He was holding me, the crippled child, in his arms. This photo does not feature my condition, but it shows a strong, caring father carrying a child he loves. My father is wearing a broad smile, as if he knew one day his namesake would walk, even if it began with a limp. It was as if he knew the generational consequences of this adversity would be strength. Dad died shortly thereafter, and I began walking. Not straight or strong, but it began with a limp.

Walking with a limp draws attention. It attracts comments from others who lack experience with your condition. Observers cannot know what you are going through; my elder sibling and others were able to walk, but limping became my lot. Emotional limping affects many parts of life, including our health and creativity. If we are not careful, it can affect our capacity to build a legacy. Limping impedes speed, but it does not halt progress. You see, even if you are limping, you are moving forward. You are pressing on toward the goal. You don't have to be graceful; you just have to be moving. We must not underestimate the power of walking with a limp.

We live in a fast-paced society where few possess the gift of patience or endurance. Bandwidth measures the speed of media, phones keep getting faster and smarter, bank tellers are being replaced by ATM stations, and social media measures accomplishments in terms of "followers." My father left his legacy by subscribing to another archaic principle called "trust and belief." It was written across his smiling face in one photo I have of him and myself. Dad Andrew carried me until he departed in death. I'm told he never looked as if he was carrying a burden or hopeless child, but his smile showed trust and belief that I would one day live a life beyond my condition. I bear his name and remain part of his legacy; so to him, any amount of limping was acceptable until walking was possible. Dad died when I was three years of age. I continued to limp up through Dad's death, but today I enjoy the masterful walk of life with my three grandchildren.

Progress is not measured by speed. It is continuous movement forward while an event or project is undergoing development. Progress is relative; it may be escalated or deescalated as development continues. Limping in life is a humbling, weakening process visible to all; but few see the development taking place beneath it. Death or shattering events may leave you with an emotional limp. For me, a physical limp led to emotional limping; simple childhood tasks became burdensome, and I was confined to a room while others ventured outside. Being alone for extended periods of time also contributes to emotional limping. But I will tell you this: Limping is better than stagnation. The latter leads to surrender; limping starts progress.

Determination and Focus

Some innate power forced me not to accept the word *crippled* but not *lame*. Perhaps it was Dad's unspoken transfer of encouragement. Perhaps the divine order for my life required limping before walking. But I was determined not to stand idle in life or to give in to a limiting narrative.

Determination is real, transformative power; it produces change and redirection. Some were born with silver spoons in their mouths. Their *after* is greatly different than yours, because you will experience more limping moments, searching for understanding and meaningful purpose.

I came across this priceless quote during a visit to Saint Jude Children's Research Hospital. A young cancer patient wrote out these words and posted them as a reminder:

> Life is like a camera:
> Focus on what's important,
> Capture the good times
> Develop from the negatives,
> And if things don't work out,
> Take another shot.

Determination is taking another shot at life. Limping is never a fatal impairment. It simply slows progress without interrupting life. You will face barriers, whether they stem from lack of desired resources or being dropped or broken over the course of your life. In your *after,* remain sensitive to emotional valleys; we are products of disarray and trying elements. Social inequities have existed nearly since the time of creation, nation against nation, man against man, or gender against gender. *After* is a message of hope for inspired minds who seek to move forward. The book of Genesis tells us how Abraham, Sarah's husband and Isaac's father, staggered for nearly twenty-five years—a delay he caused due to his unbelief. But he still followed God's call to leave his home and move to a new land. He did not sit down and quit. Determination breeds confidence. It produces mental mobility—and a new future.

Remember Where You've Come From

Some may feel life started with a limp due to the circumstances they were born into. Do not despise your meager beginnings (Zechariah 4:10). Andrew Carnegie Turner was a man of meager means. He migrated from the South, having limited education. He vowed to leave a legacy for his children's children, and he is an inspiration to this day. Aim high in life; do not become fearful of falling. Never allow meager beginnings to determine your desired outcomes. Remember, life is never fair, but you have the gift of twenty-four hours in each day. Do not focus upon your beginnings; do not allow shattered experiences to create undesirable endings.

"You must crawl before you walk." It's more than just a cliché saying. It will be essential to your *after.* When you have become stable, strong, and established, do not be ashamed of having experienced limping moments. These challenges are tools for success, inspirational memories, or just examples of how determination has overcome your crippled beginning.

Another inspirational quote hangs upon a wall in Saint Jude Children's Research Hospital:

> Surround yourself with
> The dreamers and the doers,
> The believers and thinkers,
> But most of all surround yourself with those who see

Greatness within you,

Even when you don't see it in yourself.

Danny Thomas, the founder of Saint Jude's, was a dreamer and a doer. He began with only a few dollars in his pocket and a desperate desire to leave a legacy and honor God. It would be a legacy saying no child should die of disease while in the dawn of life. His dreaming became doing, backed by constant prayer. Eventually, through his grit and determination, he shared his passion around the country and funds were raised to build his research hospital for children. Saint Jude is the patron saint of lost causes, and today the institution bearing his name is a "beacon of hope."[12]

Our legacy building must go beyond what we leave in a last will and testament. Legacy building starts with seeing your limping as a cause for desire and determination to grow beyond your immediate circle of influence. Influence creates interest in and awareness of your life's story. Influence comes from tenacity and character, displayed in such a way that inspires others to follow in your footsteps.

My father's legacy was inspirational. He became a land owner, which others considered impossible given his blue-collar income. My grandmother was also a landowner—a self-educated widow armed with poise and class. Grandmother passed this legacy on to my father, and he passed determination to my generation. I live each day inspired to leave a legacy for my children's children. *After* unleashes the power of legacy building. No one should die without leaving tools and a legacy of determination and inspiration for their children's children.

From Limping to Running

The Boston marathon attracts runners from around the world, from elite athletes to those desiring to simply finish the race regardless of their position or time. Those runners are not interested in telling people what place they took at the finish; they are happy just to say they ran in the Boston marathon. And they finished.

After is not a sprint; it's a marathon race made up of diverse individuals, with different goals and backgrounds, heading toward the finish line. This race toward *after* may take hours, months, or even years. But regardless, it can be achieved with dedication, commitment, coaching, and inspiration. *After* runners must avoid becoming discouraged if the pace of recovery seems slow. Patience outweighs speed, and endurance produces a win. And all *after* seekers are winners in the end, whether we limp there, jog there, or race there.

Transformed

Moving forward begins within our transformative nature. Paul writes in Romans 12:2, "Be ye transformed by the renewing of your minds" (KJV). Transformation is a metamorphosis, when our old state of being has given way to another form. Remember the caterpillar and the butterfly. The caterpillar stays in the chrysalis anywhere between days and months, depending on the species. The caterpillar must leave ground level and risk hanging upside down until its moment arrives, and it emerges completely transformed. Mental transformation is more than just having a mind-set; it requires cutting oneself off from one state until one reaches another positive state of being.

After is transformative in the same way. It allows victims of abuse, those with stagnant lives, ministry leaders, families, business owners, or shattered individuals a very unique moment to hang still until they are ready to take flight. And when you begin to move your wings, you must be prepared to experience some trial and error. With any movement comes risk.

Risk and Failure

Fear is part of human nature. We all must contend with it, for it slows down our movement and progress. Fear breeds failure and creates another false narrative, suggesting that doing nothing is safer than risking a new beginning and that staying inside the chrysalis is safer than spreading your wings. Fear is a negative spirit housed in thoughts, ideologies, and norms. Cultures often breed fear by suggesting risk is evil or will end in failure. *After* seekers recognize the presence of fear and make a commitment to move beyond it.

Overcoming fear can result in finding new relationships and in transformative thinking. Our minds have massive capacity, exceeding any computer processor, but they can also sabotage us with fear of failure. But now you know that failure is an asset; it teaches us foundational truths about setbacks, rejections, loss of wages, loss of life, loss of a home, or loss of loved ones. Our movement in life is a series of successes and failures. Success comes through trial and error. It comes from becoming a risk taker instead of being a professional failure—or someone for whom terminal defeat has overtaken drive and persuasive determination. The professional failure's resumé reads as follows: "I lack drive, determination, aspiration, or hope. Hobbies: none. Life expectations: none. Dreams, they are nightmares. Formally educated, but formally defeated." There is no pride in being a professional failure. Instead, be a risk taker who is not defined by failures.

Mentorship is most valuable when assessing risk. Forms of mentorship like professional coaching or life coaching can encourage mobility through deliberate planning. This often includes adding a level of risk into your life. If you are able, locate a life coach who is skilled in bringing results to clients who are willing to take risks. It is worth the investment. Otherwise, invest your time in finding and reading books by coaches who excel in the area you wish to grow in. There are countless resources available, from recorded talks, articles, literature, and even online coaching, for those who look for them. If you know someone who is excelling in a way you admire, consider asking that person to mentor you for a period of time. Meet for coffee and ask thoughtful questions about their successes and failures. Learn first-hand from their experience.

My own life coach passed away three years before this book was written. She spoke volumes, showing two fatherless sons how to manage life with meager resources while nurturing inquisitive minds.

My dear mother, like our father, was a believer—which is vastly different than one who believes.

The Bible gives us a poignant distinction between a believer and one who believes. A father brought his sick son to this designated place to obtain healing for his son's lifelong condition. The disciples were not able to deliver the boy, so the father brought him directly to the Savior. He acted on his belief—making him a believer, rather than one who merely believes. A believer does not waver while facing elements of life. A believer is strategic and makes clear decisions based upon experience, while some who believe will sit inactive. A believer seeks wisdom or aid when he or she faces new challenges. Believers say to the Father, like this man did, "Help thou mine unbelief" (Mark 9:24 KJV). Jesus told him to bring the child to Him for healing, suggesting that believers act upon this foundation.

Yes, Mother was a believer—a woman of action. Mother fought for and regained her mobility following our father's death. Widowhood was her position in life, but it did not dictate her outcomes. Mother became keenly aware of her voice, her power, and her ability to inspire others. Her encouragement was forthright, strong, and deliberate. She possessed drive and ingenuity, and gave empowering insight. Her drive was phenomenal up until her death. She never embraced fear, but rather sought new opportunities. She embedded these values within my brother and myself. He later became a very successful business owner, and I explored aerospace and launched my first company. We learned, from her, to live with risk!

Michael Jordan said that failure should be fuel for success: "I can accept failure. Everyone fails at something. But I can't accept not trying."[13] Certainly his risks and failures have resulted in a legendary career and iconic status.

Another sports icon, the Nike company, has embraced a brand slogan that is indelible in our culture: "Just Do It." This phase was actually inspired by the last words of a man facing a firing squad, which were recorded and reported in a Portland paper. The words stuck in the mind of an advertising executive, who worked them into a now-famous ad campaign in 1988. It is "arguably the best tag-line of the twentieth century" because it can mean many things to many people—and to us, seekers of *after,* it speaks to recovery and comeback.[14] You have survived severe attacks, and now is the time to "just do it"—just stand up and live your best life now. Move. Risk. Spread your wings.

Standing Despite Unfairness

Have you ever felt progress was foreign? Have you considered surrendering because of unfair events? In these moments, please stand. Having done all you can, just stand. Let us review concepts for overcoming these less than fair moments. Standing is the key!

We all must reach a decisive point where we get beyond inequities in life or we might become entrenched in a dark past. Part of this is accepting that bad things do happen to good people. To those who would say, "You reap what you sow," I have a desperate question: Did those who tragically died on 9/11 sow miserable seeds in life that caused them to die in a terror attack? Did my mother, an upright woman who kept a vigil before God, deserve to die from cancer? Do the countless merciless murders in America, including those in the Las Vegas shooting, come as a result of the victims' devastating deeds? We cannot truly accept our *after* until we know that our Father grieves at these ills, but He also restores after the devastation.

This is a matter of acceptance. It is not a debate about the goodness or existence of God. There is purpose in our lives. As I speak here to believers, I encourage non-believers to accept that all things have purpose.

"After you've done all you can, you just stand." Marvin Sapp, Marvin Winans, and Donnie McClurkin are just three modern-day psalmists who have transformed these lyrics into a gospel classic.[15] Yet this song is more than a song. It continues the powerful command needed to reach your *after.* If we cannot run, walk, or limp, we must stand—and live on.

We are standing, powerful individuals, and I encourage you to realize our Father has built us to last. Perhaps you have survived battles, sickness, bankruptcy, divorce, abuse, disease, loss of spouse, loss of finances, or loss of ministry, but you are yet standing—facing not another storm but a place and position reserved for the victorious ones who have moved into *after*.

Perhaps good is only relative to our Creator as He looked back at His creation and declared it was good. In our limited sight, bad often overshadows the good. But as Romans 8:28 encourages us, "we know all things work together for good to them that love God, to them that are called according to his purpose" (NIV). "All things" includes desired and undesired, good and not good, healthy and unhealthy, kind and unkind, friendly and unfriendly, loving and hateful, calm and furious, warlike and peaceful, with plenty and with lack.

To clearly grasp this, make a list of your "unexpected realities"— the things that taught you about unfairness. You may well know that pain, disappointment, deception, hurt, heartache, and mistrust are true realities in our world. But how could God be working "all things" in your favor? Your list may look something like this:

Dreams	Unexpected Realities
Complete all academic pursuits	College tuition exceeds your budget
Secure executive-level position with six figure income	America enters the Great Recession in 2008
Wonderful spouse with the wedding of your dreams	Post-marital counseling and a hefty child support bill
Start new business	Investors abandon project
Thriving, financially sound ministry	A painful church split, filing for bankruptcy protection, laying off staff members

I am certain you have a list of good versus evil. Read it one last time and write beneath it these simple words: "But I am still standing." And beside each reality, pray for guidance to see how God will use it in the future to help you move forward.

This subject is close to my heart following a seven-year period when unexpected realities seemed to come without ceasing. I suffered incomprehensible physical pain from neck surgery that was unmanageable without heavy medication. Emotional pain quickly followed when two of my spiritual sons sought to orchestrate a church split during my recovery from surgery. All too soon my bride succumbed to cancer after nineteen months of caretaking in our young marriage. Two days after her burial, lawyers, insurance representatives, and human resource professionals presented me with yet another pain: the insurance she carried had been cancelled and the car payment I made on the car she drove was never hers. It was all so unfair. In the onslaught, anger was a temptation, but I had to move from asking "Why?" into planning for *after*. The difference between my dreams and realities was staggering, but I had to trust that God had a plan, and continue to stand. Finally, I was able to move forward.

Get Up and Walk

If at any point in this *after* journey you have felt paralyzed, unable to move ahead, you are in good company. And sometimes, of course, being still is necessary to rest and recuperate. But there comes a time when, like the paralytic Jesus healed in Mark 2, we must "get up ... and walk" (v. 9).

I learned much about overcoming mental paralysis by facing a period of physical paralysis. Some surgeons deemed my condition inoperable and permanent, but, thanks be to God, He provided me with a surgeon who was willing to try. He steadied the surgeon's hands and gave favor at each level. And He led me into recovery.

My recovery was slow and painful, but it was progress. When my brother came to visit me in the hospital, he had never seen me so incapacitated and immobile, having to use a walker to move into the next room. Carl, my elder brother, actually shed tears on one of his three days with me. My pain was beyond comprehension. My pain level was so high that I became delirious, with no relief in sight. I was so frequently in tears that doctors sent a pain specialist into my room to minimize the pain. The pain specialist said, "Andrew, you must get up and walk. This will cause life to come again into the damaged areas, causing the spinal fluid to flow."

Get up and walk? *He has clearly lost his mind*, I thought. I was on the highest legal dose of narcotics, and nothing was causing my pain to abate. The doctor then interjected with words I will never forget. My doctor looked directly in my tear-filled eyes and said, "You have to get up and walk. The pain will abate."

This was not the supportive advice I expected. It did not seem to take into account my current situation. I couldn't think about standing up on my weak and weary feet, with a brace around my neck. I was weak from nearly fifteen pounds lost in one week. Along with the pain, I was lonely, with no spouse to comfort me. My youngest daughter/caretaker left the room; she later said that she could not stand to see her father in that level of pain. Could the doctor's advice—"Get up and walk"—even be possible?

I've come to learn that good advice never will meet your expectations. Good advice will never come from those who merely sympathize with your plight, but from those who want what's best for you.

I wanted to hear, "Andrew, in light of your family status, your public humiliation, and your near paralysis, let's find a very comfortable bed that has pillows, a nurse, a flat screen television, and no contact with the outside world." That is what I wanted to hear, but it would have prolonged my recovery and led to other complications.

Comfort is not a sign of *after*. You must embrace being uncomfortable to a pain level that provokes standing and walking. I'm sure you know of individuals who continuously take upon themselves a victim's mentality. They rarely progress. Conversely, pain will bring tears, but if you are standing in tears it's better than crying into a pillow.

I lost my ability to write simple alphabetical letters due to weakening motor skills. My temporary paralysis was taking its toll. So the therapist began teaching me how to print my name and to learn the alphabet. This was humiliating, yet it was essential to my eventual recovery. Sickness is never kind, but we may never know the role struggles play in giving us strength in life. Going down is never defeat. It's temporary.

My doctors had little understanding of the many struggles in my life, but they approached me with the view that my life was full of possibilities. Within me was a voice greater than the pain in my neck. It reminded me of my desires, my plans, and my ability to overcome.

You must find your inner voice of truth during dark moments. This voice will contend with negativity, pain, people, and purpose. Success is never achieved without pain. *After* is not for normal people. It is for determined, self-willed, divinely driven men and women.

Your motive for recovery is not merely self-serving, but rather for a greater cause. This is not just about you alone. Younger generations want to see living proof of recovery after dire straits and hardships. Telling a compelling story in this society requires transparency about pain and hardships. Standing and walking down a sterile hospital hall with an exposed behind was not what I would have chosen, but it was a necessary part of my journey. The exposure was chilling, but as I passed others in total body casts or with feeding tubes, and some with incurable diseases, I realized that standing and walking at a slow pace had its benefits. A few weeks later, I was discharged to my home and given a cane. Using a cane may have seemed burdensome to some, but in my view, the cane represented progress.

Even if you are limping at this point in your life, even if you are exposed or in pain, or struggling to remain standing, I encourage you to get up and walk toward your future. Most if not all great men and women have been knocked down. My surgical experience left me with a six-inch scar that is not visible looking into my face, but it's clear to those walking behind me. Few people will see what you have endured while you face them, but those following will know the price you have paid. You are still on your feet!

—— ✳ ——

Reflection Questions

1. Why should we not be ashamed of walking with a limp?

_____

_____

_____

2. What does "crawling before you walk" mean in your situation? What constitutes a move forward for you?

_____

_____

_____

3. How do you hope your limping moments strengthen your legacy?

_____

_____

_____

4. What fears and failures must you move past in order to keep limping, walking, running, or even standing?

_____

_____

_____

5. What did you learn from charting your dreams and unexpected realities? How can you take pride in still standing?

_____

_____

_____

6. Do you believe that all things are working together for your good? How does this affect your faith?

_____

_____

_____

7. In what ways might "getting up and walking" after an injured period, emotional or physical, bring new life to you? What is stopping you?

_____

_____

_____

CHAPTER 12

You Are Built to Last

Southern California is breathtaking in its natural beauty. Our majestic mountains seem to have been sculpted by an artistic hand. The weather is consistently pleasant, making our region an oasis for tourism. Our valleys benefit from daily sunshine, while snow rests upon soaring mountain peaks in winter months. Still, we are not immune to nature's extremes. Fierce seasonal wind storms occur each year, often causing severe damage and raging forest fires that destroy homes, property, and sometimes life itself. After a forest fire, though, we see something remarkable: the renewal of life. It amazes me to see miles of charred mountains, seemingly desolate terrain laying silent as if life has ended. But then, life begins to return.

Recent fires in our area caused highway closures, as wind pushed flames from one eastern mountaintop to the west side, leaving nothing but ashes and smoke. Smoke plumes have risen thousands of feet into the air, blocking out sunrays and affecting residents with asthma. But without fail, each year the burn areas soon become radiant with new life. The greenery and new foliage might leave some surprised to know that wind and fire had destroyed this area at all.

Along with the resilient terrain, our wildlife has learned to thrive in these conditions. A mother and father blue jay once decided to build their nest in an evergreen tree outside my patio. The process was meticulous; each day new twigs were interwoven inside this tree. They completed the nest just before a period of fierce wind storms. My heart went out to them; I thought they'd surely be lost when winds reached over sixty miles per hour. Trees were falling, shingles tumbled from rooftops, but these blue jays never moved or wavered. They sat unbothered upon their nest while fierce winds tumbled trees and blew masses of debris. The blue jays seemed to know that a greater, better life was coming after this storm. To my amazement, their stability produced another beautiful blue jay as the mother rested firmly inside the nest. She remained strong, sitting atop her egg, perhaps knowing that it would one day hatch and take flight because his mother sat strong through this storm.

Life's winds will blow, but the blue jays offer a vital lesson: stay in the nest until the storm winds subside. Just like the natural landscape of Southern California, life springs anew *after* the storm. Bloom brightly in your *after,* giving inspirational courage to motivate others, giving them hope that they will withstand their own winds and fires until new life begins. It will begin; this promise is true. If not today, hold firm until tomorrow.

We can all gain strength and inspiration from the legendary personalities we see memorialized in print or on screen. But *after* is the epic story of those who may have little or no footprint in society. These are individuals who, like blue jays and the mountains, have weathered storms and found *after.* They are not listed in *Who's Who.* The do not appear before sold-out arenas to unpack their stories. *After* is for you, the everyday person, regardless of age, background, ethnicity, failure, or success—because you possess a spirit and tenacity greater than blue jays sitting in a nest enduring wind gust beyond comprehension. You are faced with the decision to take hold of a better way of life in your *after.* Make this decision without procrastination. You have endured turbulent storms, but they have prepared you for greatness. As the California mountains take on new life, so shall previously shattered men and women.

Expect a Better Life

"Behold, I will do a new thing; now it shall spring forth; shall
ye not know it? I will even make a way in the wilderness, and
rivers in the desert." (Isaiah 43:19 KJV)

This Old Testament prophetic promise was given to Israel following their severe grief, anguish, sickness, and moments of uncertainty. They had learned to expect the worst. The nation had turned away from divine guidance to follow after trends and idols. But now, returning to the Lord, they were being asked to hope. To trust. To obey.

The best promises of life are found through trust and unwavering obedience, even when all hope seems lost. I firmly believe in this simple concept, presented by Isaiah in this passage of Scripture. A new life for you shall arise out of these ashes. It's promised. Our lives are products of divine order. Those seeking *after* recognize the power of purpose, and we truly believe *greater* is coming. California fires are nature's way of removing foliage, allowing moisture, sunshine, and time to produce green pastures on land that seemed dead to our eyes. The seeds were never burned in these fierce fires; they were forced deeper beneath the soil, forming deep roots. The seeds were not disturbed by wind or fire because the natural order preserved them. Your *after* springs from the seed lying buried in your soul. Your will to live a better life comes from a deeper divine order. Like the blue jays and the mountains, you can become stronger in the fierce moments of life.

Built Tough

Ford uses a wonderful slogan for its trucks: "Built Tough to Last." We know trucks depreciate from day one and lose value over time.

But you are built tough to last in a different and better way. You grow stronger with time. And your Father made you that way—to endure.

The things that make a truck "built tough" are surprisingly similar to the things that make you tough: power, consistency, durability, and the ability to transport heavy loads.

First, consider *power*. In a truck it might come from a turbo diesel engine. But for us, knowledge is power. It produces wisdom, inspires creativity, and drives us to seek outside input, like fuel for the engine, so that a new life will become your reality and not a far-off dream. Seek knowledge from books; Rick Warren's *The Purpose Driven Life* is a must-read, among others listed in the resources section at the back of this book. Seek knowledge from courses, coaches, mentors, others you admire, experts in their field, and online resources. Find out more about yourself and more about the situation you wish to inhabit. Make plans, and back them up with the power of knowledge.

Next, there's *consistency*. A solid truck is one you can depend on— one that starts and performs consistently. Consistency is vital for your *after* as well. Sustained increase often does not come from luck or from massive efforts but rather from consistency. Daily dependability is vital when one is reaching *after*. Each day is newly full of opportunities—and of opposition. Let's undermine opposition by remaining strong: outline your goals, and write down the new habits you will need to develop and maintain to reach your definition of success. Three of the most important, most indispensable habits you will need for any goal are prayer, planning, and participating. Each day, spend time in prayer, in planning the use of your time, and in participating in life's activities and connecting with others. Consistency doesn't just happen; it is built one day, one decision at a time.

Durability is structural soundness—it's stability against the elements. A durable truck's bumper doesn't fall off when it hits a speed bump. In us, durability starts with patience. For us, durability is patience. Many of us find "patience" to be a trying word. Most don't like to wait for a good outcome but rather come apart at the onset of any challenge. But a durable person displays confident patience. The difference between waiting and displaying patience is clear. Waiting leaves room for doubt; it creates weariness, causing instability and insecurity. Waiting with patience shows confidence in one's goals, backed up with the knowledge required to withstand another level of living. For instance, when you build a brand for yourself, others begin to recognize what makes your brand unique. They observe your behavior, responses, and verbal and nonverbal communication styles. Behavior speaks to character and strength. Take inventory of your reactions to delays in your plans and contracts, to business deals, to leadership in ministry, or to trying family situations. Are you sound and stable like the blue jays in the wind, or is there a temptation to abort and fly away? Are you patient and durable? Or do you fall apart at the merest speed bump? Display durability with patience, because you were built to last.

Finally, we consider load bearing. Perhaps you have carried heavy loads. You have been hauling more in this life than even the strongest truck was built to haul. The life and days of great men and women will often include moments when you simply say you have had enough, a place where you have reached an overload in every way. Perhaps this came after a great loss of a loved one, a marriage, ministry, or financial crisis. This is reality for many who have seen inequities in this life; however, looking back, you now can simply say, "I was built to last." A heavy load wasn't meant to stay in the bed of your truck forever but to be transported to where it belongs and unloaded. Believer, to lighten your load, know that "all things are working together" for our good.

Bringing *After* to the Generations

No discussion about life *after* would be complete without addressing the way our actions affect future generations. *After* is not just for individuals; it offers value to each generation in our culture. Millennials tend to live for today, knowing little about financial recessions and the trials of previous generations. Generation X-ers are still gaining experience. Baby boomers and elders have the perspective of time, and many personally know the need for *after*.

That is not to say that wisdom comes with age. Unfortunately, there's no scientific evidence to support this theory. Some have aged and still lack wisdom. In reality, age is not synonymous with wisdom. Wisdom and experience are byproducts of a progressive mind-set. Wisdom suggests you are qualified to become "new" based on intentional, decisive behaviors, leaving burned areas of life for new opportunities.

A concerted, dedicated effort is needed to save our families, ministries, and communities across generations, or we will be left behind. Shaping culture can no longer be left to social workers and civic leaders. We must make an effort to transfer our basic core values deliberately throughout generations. It will not be an easy task, but it is essential to our future. To do this, we must make an effort to overcome the generation gap and pass on principles of *after*.

My brother, Carl, and I were having a dinner with our children, which was rare because we live on opposite ends of the United States. (I live in the West; Carl lives in the East.) The subject centered upon our adult children, who were having an engaging conversation and, to Carl's alarm, comparing their tattoos. Carl, being very conservative, began investigating this with deep personal convictions. He leaned toward me, asking, "Do you think your daughter has a tattoo?" I said, "Carl, no one in that generation has *a* tattoo. They have several." In disbelief, Carl rose up and asked his daughter, "Do you have a tattoo?" She quietly responded, "Yes, Daddy. I have several." My brother marched down the line with our children in dismay, seeking to understand the value of a tattoo. This trend escaped our generation, but it is symbolic of creative desires in our children. It is our duty to try to understand each other.

So many differences exist within our society. Some are easy to accept, and some we find unpleasant. Our cities are reeling as we are seeking to develop communication with members of authority who see young people as a threat. The power of community, civic engagement, and the church is greatly altered by both time and culture. Riots returned to the public eye in 2015, but their causes have been underway for decades. The unrest in society today is cross-cultural and global. African Americans and Hispanics made up less than 32 percent of America's population in 2015, but they were nearly 56 percent of the population of correctional institutions.[16] These disproportionate values are affecting dreams, desires, and aspirations on all levels. We need to find an *after* for our society.

Social and economic concerns affect religious leaders and families alike. Religious leaders are struggling with how to effect change, life, and growth in the community while membership continues to decline. The days of staying in church for more than two hours are gone. Many people are now asking, "Do I need a church to foster my relationship with an ever-present God?" Countless ministries are struggling with consistent downturn in attendance and contributions. We must not disengage during these critical times of unrest, injustice, and decline. We must stay the course in our communities, repeating the message that *after* is possible for groups and societies as well as individuals. *After* may look different than the present, and may require new and creative solutions, but it is possible. We must remain open to each other and not give up hope.

After for the Church

The longer I live, the more it becomes apparent to me that life is changing quickly in places where it used to be stable. As we become more distractible in life, susceptible to messages coming at us from all angles, we become more distractible in our purpose as a church. That purpose is to spread the good news of Christ and all the while "encourage one another and build each other up" (1 Thessalonians 5:11). It is to be the hands and feet of Christ to the world. And, as Ephesians 4:12 tells us, "Christ himself gave the apostles, the prophets, the evangelists, the pastors and teachers, to equip his people for works of service, so that the body of Christ may be built up." It is a holy, worthy calling. We miss this calling, however, when we focus on pursuits that fail to build one another up, in leadership and across generations and communities. We must, as a church, find an *after* in these areas.

The key is to remain focused on our purpose, regardless of the volume of waste placed before you. And if you are a committed church member or leader, you will undoubtedly encounter such waste. I heard an amazing story from a minister who said he saw me entering a hotel elevator in South Jersey with a young female. He said that he later called my room to tell me to be careful of whom you pass when entering an elevator. Was this in fact a fellow believer, "building me up" and encouraging me toward holiness in leadership? Not likely. First of all, our hotel didn't even have an elevator. And second, he did not know the lady accompanying me that day was my adult daughter, who affectionately still holds my hand in public though she is forty-one. I could have become unduly troubled by this conversation. Waste such as this can become problematic to those easily swayed, but we must not focus on it during our pursuit of *after*. We must regain the purpose of the church—for building up, not tearing down.

After will never be acquired without sweeping away garbage, distrust, and unproductive conversations. Struggling against the negativity and distrust of others saps your energy and gives untold strength to those who target you. When you are a visible champion of *after*, you have to live through everything thrown into your pathway. Consider Job. He was noted for being upright, wealthy, and socially balanced, and this made him a target for adversity. Job's capacity was demonstrated not by the loss of his sons and daughters, the cattle, camel, maids, or his burning property. His capacity was demonstrated when the Creator allowed Job's wife to live and then insult him by asking, "Why don't you curse God and die?"—and Job refused (Job 2:9). Like Job's wife, those remaining adversities are sometimes left to push you into the final phase called success. We must take them as cues to refocus on what matters—to refuse to curse God and die.

Distrust within the church is not our only hurdle to cross. We need to build trust between the church and the community. Our most basic questions must be: What is the true relationship between church and community? How do we provide a message to a generation with increasing technology and decreasing theology? Does the local church have the capacity to enter into today's life effectively?

Complaining about differences, such as tattoos upon the bodies of our young adults, will not lead us into an effective *after* as a church and community. We have to address civic engagement while developing policy to provoke lasting, uplifting change in our communities. Development, creativity, independence, and engagement is the new theme for success in today's social and economic circles. Having a sermon without a plan is no longer acceptable. Leaders must surround themselves with key contributors or vital talents who possess vocational abilities that go beyond the pulpit.

Ministry must remain relevant or its messaging will become stale, lost, or irrelevant to those it seeks to reach. Shifting cultures, norms, and values are major contributors to this vocation called ministry. Ministries must not be afraid to break tradition and present programmatic ideas to enhance community, providing social, economic, and health benefits and services. For instance, church health fairs now address mental health, family, and other touch points. The staff must provide relevant insight to the ministry, including finance, fitness, family, and health. A healthy church will include all ages, which suggests it is relevant. A biased or irrelevant church will exclude ministry that reaches the hearts of future members, not just those in attendance.

Planning is critical and essential to this journey, and you must plan for rejection, refusals, returns, and denials while on the road to *after*. Embrace these elements, and remember that your pain produces perfected products. The church was built to last; we are told that it was built on a rock, and the "gates of Hades will not overcome it" (Matthew 16:18). We seekers of *after* must keep building it in ways that will last beyond our lifetimes. We can do this because we ourselves were built to last—"being strengthened with all power according to his glorious might so that [we] may have great endurance and patience" (Colossians 1:11).

Reflection Questions

1. If your life has recently experienced a forest fire, what seeds are beginning to grow from it?

   _____

   _____

   _____

   _____

2. Do you believe that your Father built you tough, to last? How can you change the things you say to or think about yourself to reflect this fact?

   _____

   _____

   _____

   _____

   _____

3. How will you seek the power of knowledge moving forward into your *after*?

   _____

   _____

   _____

4.   What can you do in your daily life that will help you maintain a consistent commitment to the changes you have decided to make during the course of this book?

_____

_____

_____

5.   Where can you grow patience in your life? In what ways will it be essential in your particular journey toward *after*?

_____

_____

_____

_____

6.   How do you plan to contribute to an intergenerational *after*?

_____

_____

_____

7.   As a member of the body of Christ, the church, how will you promote the principles of *after* in your congregation and community?

_____

_____

_____

_____

The Beginning of Your *After*

Adversity made me better, not bitter. It is with this simple principle that I wish to leave you. The preceding chapters sought to align two extreme elements, death and life, into a very unique posture called *after*. Death attaches itself to life, creating overwhelming constraints, stagnations, and the very things that stop us from being our best selves. These chapters explored death's impact upon us. Emotional death, financial death, marital death, and societal death each affect us in different ways. Ministry leaders are weathering death. Church members, executives, workers, mothers, fathers, and family members—the young and old are, too. But there is life *after* death.

Bitterness makes us withdrawn, breeding captivity. I wrote *After* to inspire *betterness* instead. It provokes "a new you" and leads to *after*—a life-changing posture for those who no longer accept defeat amid negativity, stagnation, or shattered dreams.

In these pages we have explored the three stages of finding *after*: from *forgetting what is behind,* to *straining toward what is ahead,* to *pressing onward toward the goal* of renewal and freedom in this life and the next (Philippians 3:13–14). As we leave behind that which takes life, we move onward toward that which gives it.

After is dedicated to those unknown broken men and women who are willing to give life another shot, knowing they are not alone. As an *after* seeker, you refuse the invitation to settle for death or becoming a victim to adversities. You recognize your significant value and wish to transform victimization into victory. Though you may not yet feel it, you are victorious, and I know you possess an innate desire for greatness. I dedicate this work to our total recovery—yours and mine!

After is simple, a two-syllable word with exponential value. It is an invitation to find an elusive future. Too many professionals, religious leaders, business associates, and families do not know that a place called *after* exists. Countless remain unfulfilled due to their unresponsiveness to *after's* invitation. But like any invitation, it does not force itself upon shattered men or women; we must accept and embrace it.

I trust your *better* begins now.

> The God of all grace, who called you to his eternal glory in Christ, *after* you have suffered a little while, will himself restore you and make you strong, firm and steadfast. (1 Peter 5:10)

Whether you are religious or not, regardless of your denominational belief, we must accept this New Testament passage, for it offers a theological roadmap to *after*.

My niece, while editing *After*, asked two questions. "Uncle, why call this book *After*?" Second, she said this work was not of value because it lacked a viable audience. To my lovely niece: *After* is a product of determination, to all who have suffered minor to significant losses in their lives. I want them to know we have a cause, a right, and power to become greater after the loss. Lastly, I believe you know a small audience of individuals such as you who have questions and longed for answers. It's here, it's in the *After*.

A Word to Ministers on Facing Realities in Ministry

I'd like to take a moment to speak directly to those in ministry and church leadership. Because marriage and ministry are often silenced discussions in these circles, I choose to open this discussion for one reason: it's essential to finding your *after*.

Both authentic ministry and marriage are intentional efforts. You might have degrees in theology, give prolific sermons, or stand on prestigious platforms in our church culture. But who are you after the church service ends? Are you a kind, caring, fulfilled, and whole man or woman, or are you secretly shattered, searching for purpose or compassion? Where do doctors turn for care? Must they always heal themselves? Where do leaders, pastors, or their families turn when they are desperate to find *after*? It's understandable that senior pastors and leadership are finding exits to ministry; many find less hope for *after* than those they are feeding. Cultural norms and the need to "show strength" within leadership often prohibit rest, vulnerability, asking for help, and ultimately, recovery.

Leadership is not an all-out sprint; we all run with varying speeds. Some reach their goal or destiny in five years, while others suffer setbacks after twenty years of service. *After* starts by giving attention to your family pace or tempo; leaders must communicate at home first.

Those in ministry must begin to have honest discussions about the topic of marriage and relationships—and how ministry affects these areas. Rick Warren, a prominent pastor, leader, author, and exceptionally successful businessman, openly admitted that neither he nor his wife wanted to continue in a family structure at one point. Rick Warren and his wife Kay spoke with courage and truth about their extreme marital misery as well as the public devastations they had endured. While they eventually repaired their marriage, they made a point of opening the conversation about marriage and family and encouraging others to stand.[17]

The struggles of marriage and divorce are real within our congregations. One report tells us, "About 40 to 50 percent of married couples in the United States divorce, according to the American Psychological Association. The divorce rate among those who remarry is even higher."[18] The family is under great attack, and it's not getting easier. We must provide a place for healing and dialogue in the church and stand firmly upon values that enhance a family instead of those that destroy and weaken it.

Tools to enhance a family include respectful styles of communication. A partner's style of communication is often geared toward his or her culture outside of the marriage, but it can grow and change. Quality time is a critical asset in a marriage and family. Find time to date your spouse, and spend quality time with the family as a whole. What is the love language in your marriage? What are your children's love languages? Respect and find mutual goals and objectives. Discover his or her love language, protect each other, and never disclose domestic matters to family or friends. They remain judgmental after the war has ceased.

The wedding and marriage business in America is a nearly 72-billion-dollar industry.[19] Yet, church leaders put on these sacred gowns and tuxedos and then seek to minister to others without being fully aware of the impact and outcomes marriage has upon our personal lives. The family structure of ministers is under constant scrutiny, not just on Sunday, but 24-7-365. A former companion of mine, knowing this, once said to me, "I enjoy being in your private company, but marriage is not possible because you are a minister." I thanked her for being honest with no criticism.

We face enormous challenges and family pressures within the walls of ministry. Normality in your home is really abnormal—unless you believe your children and spouse are satisfied with sharing you with countless individuals. I come from a family of senior pastors, and many of my close associates often face personal perils within ministry. In this way, ministry is an entirely different world than business. Ministry leaders and their families have little or no privacy, leaving outsiders an opportunity to speculate and judge without facts. The life cycle of others' speculation can be everlasting, and judgments can be harsh, while in business you can improve your situation simply by producing a better product or finding a new customer.

Within E & I Systems, as president and owner, I was able to command a level of dedication and commitment from a group of dedicated employees. Conversely, I recall a close friend and confidant in ministry sharing how often he felt defeated and undermined by some on his staff, who seemed to have a tireless ability to disagree with every idea, plan, or vision he would cast. Ministry requires serving family, spouse, parishioners, and community members, and becoming an ambassador to your congregation.

Pastors, my advice is very simple and direct. The church is not our family, and the family is not the church. Neglecting either is problematic, so how do you reposition priorities while facing norms which do not readily embrace change? My heart labors heavily each time another young or developing pastor suffers loss of his family while standing before a congregation. A family requires time, love, caring, and simple presence. Your spouse is a spouse before she is a member of your flock. Your husband was your best friend and cherished love before becoming the senior pastor. Think of this slogan, which is vital to leadership's life: "Pleasing you pleases me." You never lay down at night with the congregation; respect your home and privacy by establishing critical boundaries inside your palace.

After is available and critical for pastors and those in ministry. You can find solace in our profession. Let's walk worthy of our vocation.

Further Reading for Your *After*

- Andrew Carnegie Turner II, *Dream Walker* (LifeBridge, 2006).

- Cecil Murray, *Twice Tested by Fire* (Figueroa Press, 2012).

- Gary Chapman, *The Five Love Languages* (Northfield Publishing, 1995).

- Jim Collins, *Good to Great* (HarperBusiness, 2011).

- Jim Collins, *How the Mighty Fall* (Collins Business Essentials, 2011).

- John C. Maxwell, *The Right to Lead* (Countryman, 2013).

- Rick Warren, *The Purpose Driven Church* (Zondervan, 2007).

- Rick Warren, *The Purpose Driven Life* (Zondervan, 2002).

- Samuel Chand, *Cracking Your Church's Culture* (Jossey-Bass, 2010).

- Spencer Johnson and Kenneth Blanchard, *Who Moved My Cheese?* (Penguin, 1998).

- Stan Toler and Alan Nelson, *The Five Star Church* (Baker, 1999).

- Sun Tzu, *The Art of War.*

- T. D. Jakes, *Destiny: Step Into Your Purpose* (Faithwords, 2015).

- Thom S. Rainer, *I Am a Church Member* (B&H, 2013).

- Thom S. Rainer, *Who Moved My Pulpit?* (B&H, 2016).

- Walter S. Thomas, *Hanging On by a Thread* (The Church Online, 2017).

About the Author

Andrew Carnegie Turner, II, is a senior pastor, servant leader, author, educator, accomplished business owner, certified executive-level life coach, fellow at USC Dr. Cecil Murray Center for Community Engagement, and founder and senior pastor/teacher of ACT2 Ministries and New Covenant Tabernacle in Los Angeles, California. He is an executive board member of St. Jude Children's Research Hospital Sunday of Hope, Bishop of Economic Development of Full Gospel Baptist Fellowship, and General Secretary of Henry Fernandez Ministry, Fort Lauderdale, Florida.

He is a native of Washington, DC, and lives in Southern California.

His greatest accomplishment is finding *after*, knowing that life is worth living beyond shattering moments.

His greatest treasures are his two adult daughters, Aneicka and Andrea Turner, and three grandchildren, Andrew Carnegie III, Adonis Kalyn, and Amora Ever-Deen.

Notes

1. Thom Rainer, "Why People Leave and How to Bring Them Back," ChurchLeaders.com, July 4, 2012, https://churchleaders.com/outreach-missions/outreach-missions-articles/138855-coming-home-why-people-leave-the-church-and-how-to-bring-them-back.html.
2. Samuel R. Chand, *Cracking Your Church's Culture Code* (San Francisco: Jossey-Bass, 2010).
3. Neel Burton, MD, "Our Hierarchy of Needs," *Psychology Today*, September 17, 2017, https://www.psychologytoday.com/intl/blog/hide-and-seek/201205/our-hierarchy-needs.
4. Roy T. Bennett, *The Light in the Heart* (2016).
5. Unattributed.
6. University of Southern California, Center for Religion and Civic Culture, "Cecil Murray Center for Community Engagement: About the Center," https://crcc.usc.edu/events-and-training/murraycenter/about/.
7. Albert Einstein, letter to Morris Raphael Cohen, professor emeritus of philosophy at the College of the City of New York, March 19, 1940.
8. Stan Toller and Alan Nelson, *The Five Star Church* (Grand Rapids: Baker, 1999).
9. Chand, *Cracking Your Church Culture*.
10. Malcolm Gladwell, "Chapter 2: The 10,000 Hour Rule," in *Outliers* (London: Penguin UK, 2008).
11. Traci Pedersen, "Childhood Adversity Affects Several Generations," PsychCentral, October 6, 2015, https://psychcentral.com/news/2013/05/06/childhood-adversity-affects-several-generations/54530.html.
12. St. Jude Children's Research Hospital, "Danny Thomas, Founder," https://www.stjude.org/directory/t/danny-thomas.html.
13. Michael Jordan, *I Can't Accept Not Trying: Michael Jordan on the Pursuit of Excellence* (San Francisco: Harper SanFrancisco, 1994).

14. Marcus Fairs, "Nike's 'Just Do It' slogan is based on a murderer's last words, says Dan Wieden," *Dezeen*, March 2015, https://www.dezeen.com/2015/03/14/nike-just-do-it-slogan-last-words-murderer-gary-gilmore-dan-wieden-kennedy/; Ashley Lutz, "The slogan that made Nike billions is inspired by a convicted murderer," *Business Insider UK*, March 18, 2015, http://uk.businessinsider.com/nike-just-do-it-inspired-by-a-murderer-2015-3?r=US&IR=T.

15. Donnie McClurken, Sylvester Stewart (lyrics), "Stand," Universal Music Publishing Group, 1996.

16. NAACP, "Criminal Justice Fact Sheet," naacp.org, https://www.naacp.org/criminal-justice-fact-sheet/.

17. Kay Warren, "Kay Warren: 'We Were in Marital Hell," *Christianity Today*, June 12, 2017, https://www.christianitytoday.com/women/2017/june/sacred-privilege-kay-rick-warren-we-were-in-marital-hell.html.

18. John Harrington and Cheyenne Buckingham, "Broken hearts: A rundown of the divorce capital of every state," *USA Today*, February 2, 2018, https://eu.usatoday.com/story/money/economy/2018/02/02/broken-hearts-rundown-divorce-capital-every-state/1078283001/.

19. Sarah Schmidt, "The Wedding Industry in 2017 and Beyond," MarketResearch.com, May 16, 2017, https://blog.marketresearch.com/the-wedding-industry-in-2017-and-beyond.